SPORT
IS MY LIFELINE

By the same author

Oliver St John Gogarty (Biography)
Brendan Behan (Biography)
Life Styles (Poems)
Ireland from 1912–1922
Three Noh Plays
Irish Tales and Sagas
The Celtic Dawn

ULICK O'CONNOR

SPORT
IS MY LIFELINE

ESSAYS FROM
THE SUNDAY TIMES

Foreword by Norris McWhirter

PELHAM BOOKS

British Library Cataloguing in Publication Data
O'Connor, Ulick
    Sport is my lifeline.
    1. Athletes—Biography
    I. Title   II. The Sunday times
    796'.092'2   GV697.A1

ISBN 0-7207-1522-9

Photoset in Great Britain by
Rowland Phototypesetting Ltd, Bury St Edmunds, Suffolk
and printed and bound by Billing & Sons Ltd
London and Worcester

These pieces were contributed to *The Sunday Times* between February 1975 and September 1982. I have to thank my editor, John Lovesey, for the encouragement he gave me and the care with which he watched over the writing of them. Much consultation, sometimes weeks of discussion, went into their preparation. It was a happy period to be working on what one felt was one of the finest sports pages of our time.

I would also like to express my gratitude to A. T. Cross for their help in the production of this collection and to Norris McWhirter for writing the foreword.

CONTENTS

ILLUSTRATIONS

Photo credits

The author and publishers are grateful to the following for permission to use
copyright photographs: Maxwells Photo Agency nos 8, 10; Times Newspapers Ltd
no. 11; Philadelphia Inquirer no. 12; John Hillelson Agency Ltd. no. 13. In some
cases it has not been possible to ascertain the copyright owner and it is hoped that
any such omissions will be excused.

FOREWORD

by Norris McWhirter

In 1951 it was Scotland's turn to be host in the annual triangular athletics international. With their superior population, the white-vested team of England and Wales always won these matches. The best that the blue-vested Scots or the green-vested Irish could do was to upset the form by taking the odd event. Undaunted by a gale blowing up the Clyde estuary into the modest stadium at Dunoon, a large but rather curious holiday crowd had assembled.

The advertised stars were all English. There was the new European 200 metre champion Brian Shenton. There was that promising miler Roger Bannister, there was the beautious Olympic silver medal winner and hurdler Maureen Gardner. It was in that wind-swept field a third of a century ago that I first encountered the green-vested Donore Harrier Ulick O'Connor wielding his vaulting pole. Among this motley assemblage it was not so much the altitude of his performance in second place as the personality which made the indelible impression.

The *dramatis personae* of the occasion are still catching glimpses of each other as life enfolds. Maureen was an early victim of cancer and her funeral was the most grief-ridden many of us will ever recall. Three years later at Oxford Bannister won immortality in less than 4 minutes. The Scots hurdler, J. G. M. Hart, transferred his domicile from Edinburgh to the City of London where he became a Sheriff. The immaculate English quarter-miler Terry (now Sir Terrence) Higgins was sworn of the Privy Council. The shot-putter Dave Guiney famous for oaths of another sort whenever he stubbed his toe on the stop board, became a larger-than-life figure in the Irish press corp. England's first 20 ft long-jumper Jean Desforges soon married that most ubiquitous and enthusiastic of television commentators, Ron Pickering. Then there was Sheila Alexander for England and the then fifteen-year-old Thelma Hopkins for Ireland who traded world records for the feminine high-jump. Among several rugby internationals competing there was one in the discus circle – the much wounded Major Charles Reidy who had packed in the second row for Ireland before the war with that legendary quadruple DSO, Colonel Paddy Maine.

For me the one who jogs the memory most often and hardest has been Ulick with the outpouring of his charming writings. With this volume he has even overcome the transitory fate of the newspaper columnist which now enables us all to re-read pieces which recapture the spirit of those rather different times.

PREFACE

The trouble about playing a lot of games at the same time is that you can break bones. At eighteen I was pole vaulting, playing rugby, boxing, and keeping wicket for a University Eleven. I would get wicket keeper's finger on a Saturday which meant that with a fractured paw I would be unable to hold the vaulting pole properly when I went out to compete the day after. Boxing didn't matter too much because if you pranged your nose you could still do other sports though I did once burst an ear drum which meant I had to spar for a while with a second row scrum cap on my head and cotton-wool in my ear. Then when I was twenty my hands got blistered after competing in a rope climbing competition in New Orleans. Next day I was doing a back flip off the horizontal bar when my hands didn't grip properly because of the blisters and I ended up in Charity Hospital near Bourbon Street having a dislocated shoulder set by a surgeon. I already had two broken collar bones from rugby. But this was different. A dislocation doesn't heal like a break and from now on I would have a game[1] shoulder. The rugby I was playing, back row forward, under twelve stone, required kamikaze tackling to make up for my lack of weight. Though I didn't know it then this would be out of the question in the future. You couldn't launch yourself at Tony O'Reilly's flying ankles with the same élan, when you had a pain like a toothache in your shoulder throughout a match, as

[1] This word is usually pronounced as 'gammy' among rugby men, a usage which may owe its origin to a Shropshire custom of pronouncing the word 'game' (to indicate lameness) in this way.

you had done before when you were all in one piece. I tried wearing a version of American football pads to cushion the crash tackle. But, apart from the hostility that this apparatus aroused in referees, I threw the pads away when a rural mite during half-time at a charity game down the country re-marked, after walking around me twice, 'I'd say that all that's there isn't yourself.'

I decided to go easy on the rugby and let pole vaulting, which I had done as a school-boy, have its chance. I had only vaulted up to this time perhaps a few weeks a year. Now I decided to take on the atrocious Irish winters of the 'fifties (there were no indoor facilities then) and vault winter and summer. I used a bucket of water to keep my hands warm so that I could grip the pole and tried not to break my neck jumping off the slippery grass take-offs. But I was twenty-two and hardy. I would convince myself that the *next* day would be dry and the wind would have fallen below hurri-cane force so that the lath would stay up. But I did miss serious Saturday rugby. Yet I told myself – this was the real thing, self discipline. Even if I hadn't the anodyne of locker-room chat and the prop of team companianship, I was on my own – like Lindbergh crossing the Atlantic. The Irish record which I held in the pole vault could easily be improved. The more it rained and hailed the more I drove my pole through the downpour, gripping it with numbed hands. But rugby had been the centre of my life since I was eight. I kept having to exorcise memories of it from my mind like a monk fighting to keep images of seductive ladies from invading his mind. It would catch me when I was off guard, even when I was asleep. In my dreams I was always making a come-back to the game. I still have these to-day. In New York, remote from rugby stadia, I can wake up in a sweat after a dream in which I have played a blinder coming out of retirement to dazzle the spectators; or there is a particularly exhausting one where I know I can really make that come-back but as I try to get to the football ground I keep getting delayed – cars, trains, taxis break down – and when I do get to the pavilion I find I have left my boots behind.

One winter's day when I thought I had the rugby business whipped, I got an insight into what the game meant to me. I was standing on the runway with my pole in a corner of a field, narcissistically absorbed as one is before each attempt, in a single aspect of the vault, which distinguishes field events from the spontaneous involvement of team games. As I picked the lath up from the pit I glanced across the field and saw the rugby men go in after a match. They were moving across the top of a raised piece of hill and behind them was a red November sky which threw them into silhouette. Their togs hung awkwardly on them – plodding rather than walking. Their figures had the sort of harmony that you see in a Millet painting: dappled beauty, 'counter, spare, strange', rather than the aesthetic perfection of limbs required if you were to shoot your body off a pole into the beckoning blue. It got me for a second and I knew I had let something slip that wouldn't return.

I blame Leni Reifenstahl for a lot of it. Her film of the Berlin Olympics had overwhelmed me. It was a massive hymn to Nordic romanticism. Rugby appeared a disorganised pastime when you came out after watching this recreation of the Attic ideal. I saw the film four times when I was eighteen and wanted to master every event in it. (Needless to say, the following season I competed in the Irish Decathlon championship.) If a similar genius had made a film on rugby I don't think I would have banjaxed my shoulder on the horizontal bar three years later. My mind had been seduced with the image of those flying gymnasts framed against the sky which were a feature of Reifenstahl's film and which gave it its moments of lasting beauty.

I had had the rugby virus injected into me very early indeed. From the age of six I had gone to matches with my father, Vice President of the University College, Dublin, Rugby Club. My grandfather also took me to games. He had played scrum-half for Blackrock in the 1880s and had early on inculcated my mother with due reverence for the game of games.

The school I was sent to looked on rugby as second to religion but only just. There were three schools in Ireland at that time run by the Holy Ghost Fathers – Blackrock, St Mary's (my one) and Rockwell. This order was originally a French one whose priests came to Ireland in 1860. Rugby at that time was dominated by the Anglo-Irish Protestant ruling class but the French priests decided to change all that. Blackrock won the Schools Cup in the first year it was put up in 1882 and since then have won it 56 times. At a Holy Ghost school rugby was studied as a science. The timing of the pass, scissor switches, the advantage line, dummies, the mechanics of these were discussed by the Fathers at Community meals with the thoroughness that they brought to advanced theological problems. The Holy Ghost Fathers are a missionary order and some of the older priests had served in fever-ridden swamps in Sierra Leone or had tramped in the tingling air in the shadow of Kilimanjaro. But even out of Ireland their minds were turning over on rugby conundrums and they returned to their Irish schools freshened by their experiences, with new solutions for getting the oval ball over the line. Whether the French Fathers had ever heard of Thomas Arnold or not they certainly used his ideas. Formation of character was the justification at these schools for the obsession with rugby. If you didn't tackle or go down on the ball you were regarded as a sort of moral leper. Boys who possessed immaculate side steps, natural swerves, and who could kick a ball half the length of the field, if they didn't show equal enthusiasm for the less glamorous side of rugby were held in universal contempt. There was also the idea around that you could learn through rugby, that no battle was ever lost if you were prepared to draw on your spiritual bank account.

Actually this sort of thinking was essential in a school as small as our one. It had closed down during the First War and was only gradually building up its numbers after re-opening in 1928. Somehow or other its teams seemed small-boned and fragile compared with those of the rival day school in the northside of the city where they had managed to attract a fair proportion of publicans' sons, beefy youths who propped up their front rows. We learned the skills early on. At ten I knew how to tackle, pass and kick and was used to two sessions a week of blackboard instruction on the game. You started in the under eights, a gaggle of untidy mites traipsing across the city on trams with rugby boots hanging round our necks herded by rosy cheeked scholastics in clerical collars who were our coaches. We played two matches a week, on Wednesdays and Saturdays, one at home and the other away. First, you were on the under eights, then the under nines, then the under tens, the under elevens and the under twelves. When you reached the under thirteens you were in the big time. Now there was a competition against Blackrock for a Cup which involved six matches. When I was eleven we took this Cup from 'Rock for the first time. In the final we were six nil down with five minutes to go when the priest who was training us took out the scrum half (later a distinguished golf international) who was minute and had been subjected to harsh treatment from surly youths on the opposite side, and changed me to that position. First of all I snatched an easy ball that had come out on the opposite side of the scrum near the Blackrock line and tipped it down. Then in the last few seconds I saw an opening and kept on running till I reached the line. The try was converted and we won. That evening, after an exquisite two hours in the bath at home, followed by a gargantuan tea, I received a call from the school. Would I come down? Now such an invitation was most unusual. The Fathers belonged to a semi-monastic order: they lived under vows of poverty, chastity and obedience and wore soutanes and cinctures. After the boys had gone home for the day they settled into a monkish regimen which included the chanting of Compline and Matins in their private chapel. The world of their remote ritual seemed as exotic to us as the goings-on in a Buddhist monastery. But when I came down to the school there was a priest waiting in the hall for me outside the Fathers' refectory. Now I was to be brought behind those walls where their secret lives were lived out. As I walked along what seemed to me endless corridors I noticed the highly polished floors with their odour of wax. This was mixed with a smell I recognised as a blend of incense and a faint aroma of chalk which I sometimes noticed emanating from the priests' soutanes. In the Refectory they were waiting for me like Elders in the Temple.

'Well, boy,' the president said, 'tell us what happened.'

They knew, of course, but they wanted to hear it in my own words to see if I had got the message. The president had a seraphic smile on his face. I had learnt my lesson. Nothing was impossible if you really believed it could be done. There was also an implication too that the Holy Ghost was not acquainted with the whole deal as a result of a crash sales job done by the Community that morning at Matins.

Later, another sports figure was to imbue me with a similar philosophy, but this time with an existential rather than a religious base. It was Franz Stampfl who coached Roger Bannister through a four minute mile and was to inspire Chris Brasher to win an Olympic medal in the steeple-chase.

'St John of the Cross,' he told me, 'could elevate himself four feet off the ground without a pole. You have something to help you upwards. Why don't you use what St John had, to do the rest?'

What Stampfl was getting at was that if you drew on your imaginative resources you would overcome merely physical limitations and improve your performance. The trouble was that St John hadn't begun whatever training he had to be a mystic by acquiring a complexity of bad reflexes. I had started pole-vaulting with a bamboo pole held together with steel wire and used to jam the instrument into a hole dug in the ground instead of sliding it into a box to commence a jump. I would approach the lath in a sort of curve like a Fosbury high jumper and as I wasn't high jumping this wasn't a very successful method of getting into the air. One day Franz convinced me that, despite the technical faults I was trying to remedy, if I used 'my creative imagination' I could vault two feet higher no matter what happened before I took off. I was so much under his spell that I took him at his word though the sceptic in me was registering negatives.

I held the pole a foot higher than I had ever held it before, came in with my curved run and atrocious plant, did everything right in the air but without enough momentum to bring my steel pole up to the vertical, landed in the vaulting box instead of the pit, and broke my ankle.

Franz was an extremely handsome Austrian who, like all Viennese, seemed to have read every book that was ever written. As a boy he had had a mystical experience in the Vienna Woods. He had pared a branch down until it became a sharp pointed javelin. Then he launched it into the air. Some energy flowed through him as it left his hand and seemed to lift it up into the sky where it floated with exquisite loneliness against the blue vault. He experienced a sort of ecstasy as he watched it descend towards his closest friend who was unaware of its flight. The perfection of what he had done so transfixed Franz that he was unable to inform his friend of the proximity of the javelin which was about to transfix *his* breast. Fortunately, it was not a serious wound but the memory of that sudden burst of untapped force remained with him when he began to coach athletics in Northern Ireland and Britain after the War.

His gospel influenced many for he was not an elitist and would coach every sort of athlete. But the three most famous protégées were Roger Bannister, Chris Brasher and Chris Chataway.

I remember Roger as a very slim medical student, his hair blowing over his face as we crossed on the ferry to Dunoon for the Triangular International between Ireland, England/ Wales, Scotland and England/Wales in 1951. Though Roger was only a few months away then from his world record, he was beaten in the half-mile that day. The following May, a week before his final medical exams, he broke the four minute barrier that some people believed would result in the human body bursting apart if anyone managed to run that fast. On the ferry to Dunoon he had talked to me about this familiar conflict between pain and ecstasy in the last part of the race as you came to exceed your previous best. As a fellow Stampflite I understood him immediately.

Chris Chataway was to break the world record for 5000 metres a year later at White City, beating the famous Russian Vladimir Kutz. His opponent indulged in an extraordinary tactic of bursting away on hundred yard dashes every now and then early on in the race with the intention of shaking Chris off. But Chataway stuck with him and managed to win at the tape though, as he later told me, he thought at one stage early on, his chest would burst as he stuck with Kutz, knowing that if he let him go he could never catch him again. It was agreeable to visit Chris in his flat and find him in his dressing gown at 10.30 am smoking a cigarette or with a glass of gin by his table. Stampfl didn't mind drinking or smoking in moderation. It was his athletes' ability to draw on the untapped spirit that counted.

Chris Brasher had the ability to do this more than any athlete I have ever known. I had once said to Franz,

'Of course, Brasher hasn't much natural ability, he only trains hard.'

Stampfl looked at me with a mixture of amusement and disdain.

'That's typically Irish. The ability to train hard is a natural talent in itself.'

In fact, Brasher was the only one of the three to win an Olympic Gold Medal. He stayed with Franz Stampfl for three months before the Melbourne Olympic Games and ran thirteen seconds faster in the steeple-chase final than he'd ever run before.

Boxing was a sport where I found you could best summon up this untapped energy. You had to if you were against the ropes and getting pounded into a pulp by some ferocious pug. The first time I was ever in the ring I had three bouts in one night (the last at 1 am). Exhausted after the second fight against the ex-welterweight champion of the Indian Army (it was 1947 and a lot of students had come up to university after serving in the War) I went out for a walk on Galway Pier to get some fresh air before the last bout. I remember lying on the canvas in the second round, not as a result of being knocked out but from sheer fatigue. Yet in the third round I managed to pull it off, summoning strength from some-where outside me through fright or maybe, now that I think of it, vanity. An early lesson on how to get outside what you thought were your limits.

It is hard now in post-welfare society to recall the stratification of the classes in the 'forties. Boxing was *one* means by which you could break down barriers. I remember going to the Battersea Boxing Club in London to ask if I could train with their lads at Latchmere Baths and getting an enthusiastic welcome. When I came out into the boxing arena there was a web of ropes stretching right across the floor of the gym which made up sixteen different rings. Boxers stepped from ring to ring as they acquired new opponents. On either side of the gym on long rows of raised seats sat *afficionados* who offered cheerful Cockney encouragement to the different fighters in the rings. You might have as many as six spars with different boxers on the same night.

What impressed me at the time (as it did in the working class gyms in Dublin – Corinthians, St Andrew's, Arbour Hill – where I also sparred) was that there was no reverse snobbery. No one gave a damn where you came from as long as you took your punches and played the game. This last aspect was most important. Boxing is, in my view, one of the last amateur sports where gentlemen's rules still obtain. I never knew a fighter to take an unfair advantage when I cruised the boxing gyms. The ritual after a fight is almost oriental. The boxers shake hands with their opponents' seconds, then with each other and after that with the referee. This spirit continues to-day. Only last year I chatted to the English flyweight after the International between England and Ireland at the National Stadium in Dublin. He was mystified by the controversy over dirty play in rugby which was causing headlines in the Press.

'Blokes kicking each other in the head, punching with bare fists. I'nt a game, is it?'

I took up soccer on account of a girl. She had represented a continental country at the Olympics in the high jump and, although she was only nineteen had retired as she thought the event would put her legs out of shape. In the meantime she seemed to have read everything worth reading about contemporary films, poetry and theatre. I had retired from competitive vaulting but it was agreeable now to train in a Paris suburb with someone who could talk about Camus and Sartre as passé, in between skimming the lath with an elegant straddle. 'Mais où sont les neiges d'antan?' Such seasons aren't made to last. Now I was faced with another exorcism – to get mademoiselle out of my system. Pole vaulting had diluted my passion for rugby. If I could find a new sport it might do the trick this time. I talked to Sean Thomas, the coach of the famous Bohemian football team. He very decently agreed to let me train with the side at Dalymount Park. At school I had refused to watch soccer in my fanatical loyalty to the oval ball game. My journey across the Liffey to Dalymount Park was not, therefore, without an element of Enrico Quarto's penitential visit to Canossa. I enjoyed the training immensely and the acquisition of new skills in a sport where my game shoulder didn't count, as this was a sport of the feet. Then, one summer Shamrock Rovers asked me to play in a series of invitation matches with them when their left wing was injured. Later that year I found myself selected on an Old Ireland team against an Old England team in Dublin before a crowd of thirty thousand at Dalymount Park. Several current internationals were playing, Ron Flowers, Jim Meadows, Graham Leggett.

My opposite number was Stanley Matthews. When I was a boy he had penetrated even my rugby orientated consciousness as a remote and majestic figure whom one conceded to be the greatest attacking player in any ball game. Now I was his opponent on the left wing. It was like being asked to mark Hermes. I worked out a plan with Tommy Eglinton, the former Everton and Ireland player, that one of us would take Stan on either side to make sure he didn't beat us with his famous body swerve.

But he strayed away from us and in the second half there was a colossal roar from the crowd on the other side of the field as he did his thing. The Irish international, Shay Keogh, described it to me afterwards.

'I went in on him, carefully, as I knew about his swerve. Suddenly I was running in the wrong direction.'

I had come full circle out of the handling code of football to the one from which it had evolved. I was now forty-four and it was time to quit taking up new sports. I still find myself from time to time walking in the street with my hands held in the position for carrying the pole or picturing myself in the air waiting for that delayed pull – or side stepping a lamp post on the way to the line.

I have no regrets for having had a go. My appetite for different sports has left me with a fitter body, I think, than if I'd just done one. There are breaks here and there in the frame, but they have held together. It is not the greatest physique to have in the world but the best to be going along with.

ATHLETICS

Pole trouble

The latest vaulting pole when it bends at take off, curves like a banana. The idea is that the curve on the pole will give extra power to spring the vaulter towards the bar. The height a vaulter can reach could from now on be determined in laboratories by industrial chemists.

I feel strongly about this fiddling with the pole because I came out of the bamboo era. When the bamboo pole curved it usually didn't straighten out again. There would be a splintering sound as you careered through the air (hopefully in a somersault) with one half of the pole in your hand.

I suppose it was some consolation to remember that fifty years before vaulters had used ash poles. When these broke the guy was often impaled. The jagged part where the pole split could remain upright to receive the falling vaulter. At least we didn't have to ask to be taken down.

Then one day bamboo was out and Swedish steel was in. The steel pole had no give at all. Vaulters who changed to it nearly had their arms torn off. You wondered if the Venus de Milo had been a pole vaulter. Then just when my arms were beginning to get used to the strain of the steel I met Ireland's greatest living poet, Patrick Kavanagh, in Grafton Street. He wrote sport on the side.

'You're finished,' he whinnied emphatically. 'I have just come from the White City and they have a new fibre glass pole. It bends in half and fires you over the bar. It's not a vault any longer. It is a bloody catapult. They're in orbit.'

He was right, I was finished. I had gone from bamboo to steel. That was enough. I couldn't change a third time to fibre glass.

Giving up vaulting had one consolation. You wouldn't have to cart your pole around any more. It was 16 feet long. The Irish Athletic Association were not well off in those days and there were seldom team buses available to carry a vaulter's pole.

When you arrived at Euston the first thing to do was to find a pillar to hide your pole behind. Then you hailed a taxi. As you moved off you would reach out the window, grab the pole and hold it against one of the door handles, while you kept your other hand in your ear so as not to hear the driver's language.

Manchester taxi drivers would not take your pole on any account. They would frequently make suggestions as to what to do with the pole but never accept it as freight.

Then there was the problem of competing in Scotland. Those marvellous Highland Games; Scottish giants tossing the caber, their cable-like muscles strained to breaking point. Kilts twirling as the wooden-handled hammer was hurled into the keen air. The savage skirl as the pipers in their gorgeous raiment swung by. But for the vaulter the real problem was how to avoid getting his pole mixed up in the pipes. You would be just starting your run towards the jump when you would see the tip of your pole a millimetre away from the lead piper of the Glasgow Police Band. The idea of damaging bagpipes in Scotland was so frightful that you spent the rest of the evening trying to vault in between bands.

Once disaster struck. I boarded a steamer going back from a Highland Games in the Isle of Bute. Disgruntled pipers, losers in the afternoon's competitions, were playing laments on the deck. I was carrying an Ayrshire carpet I had won as well as my bag and pole. I couldn't see where I was going.

As I came on board my pole went into one bagpipe. There was a sound like a scalded cat. The piper nearly burst. Words flowed like lava. His knees began to bob up and down like cannon balls under his kilt. I pointed to some boxing symbols on my blazer. This only drove additional outraged Scots to his aid.

In the end, at the mainland, the captain escorted me off (my pole aloft) through hordes of belligerent pipers playing fiercely on their instruments.

Once I got my pole on to the tube. I couldn't find a taxi to take me to the White City stadium in London. To appear under the earth with 16 feet of pole excites attention. Even the most aloof turn a curious eye. I shot the pole swiftly through the sliding doors of the tube train between the bowler hats and the *Financial Times*.

I then told the enraged inspector that I couldn't get it out again without causing havoc. How right I was. We were miles past my stop and out in the green fields before a furious engineer succeeded in prising it out through a window.

Finally I lost my pole in Germany. Getting off at Bonn I asked the porter to give me my pole from the luggage van. I only knew one German word, the one for pole. He stuck out his tongue. I shrieked and held my arms as wide as I could to show what I was looking for. He thought I meant something else and put his hands on his ears and wagged them.

I was left on Bonn platform as the train steamed off with my pole on it in the direction of Italy. I never got it back. I thought it had been appropriated by some gondolier to ply his graceful trade on a sleepy canal. My mates took a less romantic view. There were boy scouts in the train and the general consensus was that it had been nicked to hold up one of their tents.

Next morning competing against a German team I had to borrow a pole from the opposition. Not only was it rickety but as I went up towards the bar it seemed to have a built-in squeak. Maybe one of the judges was a ventriloquist. I lost my nerve and couldn't make the final heave with my shoulders.

Vaulting fulfils a primitive instinct. For a brief moment you soar Icarus-like towards the sun. Gravity, the pull of the grave, is defied. Using rigid poles we were in direct descent from the graceful fen jumpers of Norfolk who invented the game.

But this curved thing shaped like a banana. It belongs to

5

the circus tent where they fire acrobats out of a cannon and catch them in a net.

I mean, who wants to be an athletics Sputnik, sprinting down the runway with a mobile launching pad?

9th March, 1975

'Traps' and 'lats' – the making of muscle

It was the Amateur Golf Championship which first brought weight-lifting into British sport. Up to then the idea was that weights made you muscle-bound. Then Frank Stranahan, the American millionaire, after winning the amateur title in 1947, revealed that he carried a set of weights around with him and did sessions in his hotel room after matches. As he hit the ball an atrocious length off the tee, this information put paid to the muscle-bound theory.

Sometime later McDonald Bailey, the fastest man in the world then, told me he came out of the blocks faster if he did a dozen snatches with a barbell every day. It seemed a good way to make progress in the pole vault by building up my shoulder muscles.

I looked around Dublin for a weight-lifting club. I discovered one in a garage near the city centre. Shabby on the outside, inside it was a glittering palace. The gym was a hall of mirrors. There was no direction in which you could move without seeing yourself. I had discovered Narcissus' pool.

Around the room were massive men surveying themselves in the mirrors. Most of them had weights attached which seemed big enough to topple a house. Silence except for grunts. They were building muscle. The leading cat I learned was Shamus. He was a seaman who used to spend his days on a dredger in Dublin Bay working with the weights while the sea breeze kept him cool. If the captain got shirty the crew locked him in a cabin and only let him out to take the ship back to shore when their session was complete. Shamus was admired for his 'lats'. 'Lats' was the short for latissimus dorsi.

When Shamus stood up to put his speciality on display he shed enough weights to rupture a large-sized rhinoceros. Then he glared at himself in the mirrors and his 'lats' began to swell like balloons under his armpits. This I learned is the process of pumping up. If you brought enough blood to the specific muscle area by using heavy weights, it would enlarge itself in front of you.

Other members concentrated on their 'traps'. This is the trapezius muscle at the back of the neck. When they flexed them they looked for a second like webbed reptiles.

What was the purpose of it I wondered as I spent my nights in this hall of mirrors. Were they trying to make themselves objects of sexual attraction? Not at all. In fact, many of them took lime juice as an anti-aphrodisiac. The belief was that sex diverted the flow of adrenalin that was required to make their muscles bulge, and lime juice 'kept the pecker down'.

When they had finished their training an important ritual would be enacted in the dressing room. A measuring tape was taken out and each muscle measured precisely. The result was written down in a notebook and compared with the size of the muscle before the night's training had begun.

One night they asked me would I MC at a Mr Ireland competition in Rathmines Town Hall. Attired in a dress suit which really didn't fit me now as my 'traps' had begun to bulge at the shoulders, I introduced a series of massive men to an enormous audience. In the front row was a sprinkling of military-looking men with grey moustaches and monocles who brightened visibly after I announced the first competitor.

At the top of the bill was Mr World who had come over from Britain. I met him in a tiny room off the stage. It was like being close to an elephant. He seemed to shut out the light. I told him the crowd were waiting. He was surveying with enormous admiration his bicep and didn't answer. He just turned away and went back to inspecting himself.

'What size is the bi?' I asked expertly.

'16 inches cold, 19 inches pumped up,' he muttered between clenched teeth.

It was the only thing he said that night. He proferred the 'bi' to me and I put my finger into it, where it sank in as if I'd put it into a blancmange. Mr World then lay down and assisted by two acolytes began to do bench presses with a barbell the weight of two men. After some time I suggested timidly that we go on stage. His helpers glared at me.

'He ain't pumped up enough yet.'

Eventually we got him on stage. 'Show us your "traps",' the audience howled. He stood for a second, proud in his magnificence. He was in a loin cloth glistening with oil, every muscle in his massive frame fully pumped up. He flexed his trapezius till it rose up and down like the coils of a heaving python. There were orgiastic cries of appreciation. 'Where are those "bi's"?' they shouted. He turned slowly around into profile and squeezed out a truly prodigious 'bi'. Each muscle began to appear one after another in splendid isolation. The roars went up an octave. But he was only working to his climax. An expectant quiet came over the crowd. He was settling for his virtuoso piece. He turned his back to the audience, while a floodlight played on its massive crater-like terrain. Then incredibly a solitary muscle began to run up his back like a mouse. It stopped and then ran down again. Muscle after muscle was being contracted so fast that it seemed as if a single one only was wandering. This brought low moans of delight from the crowd. Then suddenly they were on their feet howling. It was the same sound that you heard later from Beatle fans. The military gents in the front had flecks of foam on their lips.

I led him off the stage, a tolerant smile playing on his prominent lips. He had said nothing all night except to answer a question about the size of his 'bi's'. Chat had always been part of the sports I played. But in the body-building world, it looked as if, as your body grew your tongue shrank. You didn't need other human beings. The one reflected in the mirror was enough. Yet what you saw there with its bland bulk was a mockery of the shapely forms that Phidias and Myron struck from stone after they had gazed on the golden skinned victors at Olympia.

It meant selling a few suits and letting my 'traps' and 'lats' subside. But I left the hall of mirrors and instead did fifty press-ups a day for a year, gazing at the unreflecting floor.

5th June, 1975

Where hammer throwing began

To throw the hammer well you should be able to spin on your toes like a dancer, and have the strength of an Andalusian bull. These requirements suited a breed of giant Irishmen bred in the Golden Vale of Munster who were often 17 stones in weight, and who could run and jump like steers. Hammer throwers from this area won every Olympic championship, except one, up to 1936. Then the Germans took over. They had photographed the Irish throwers at the White City in 1934; then they found themselves in luck when, owing to a political dispute, no Irishmen could compete at the Berlin Games.

In Rome in 1960 John Lawlor brought a touch of the old glory back by throwing 213 ft 10 in for the best Western nation's throw of the Games. Apart from that, the Irish supremacy in the hammer event has ceased to exist.

Last Sunday I watched twelve schoolboys throw at a 'Hammerama' in Belfield Stadium, Dublin. Philip Conway, the Irish record-holder in the shot-putt, had gathered them together.

There are twenty schoolboy hammer throwers in Conway's group; during the winter they compete once every three weeks, and during the summer at least once a week. Some of them travel a long distance from the country for the competitions. Their guru is a persuasive figure. When he went to the United States on a sports scholarship Philip Conway discovered a new attitude to athletics.

'It was the winner that counted,' he says. 'You had to work to win. I try to stress for the boys the importance of the maxim that significant effort will bring significant results.'

When he coached the hammer at Springfield, Massachusetts, Conway found that the heroes of the athletes he was
coaching were Dr O'Callaghan, Bert Healion and John
Flanagan. He determined to return to Ireland and revive the
lost tradition. These days he is a physical education teacher at
Belvedere College, where James Joyce was once a pupil.

The hammer throw is the one purely Irish event in the
modern Olympic programme. Though it is mentioned in
accounts of the Tailtean Games which were held in County
Meath around 300 BC, it was not included on the schedule of
the original Greek Games.

The fine techniques of the hammer-turn were evolved by
the 'Irish Whales' in New York – John Flanagan, Matt
McGrath and Paddy Ryan. Those enormous policemen all
won Olympic championships. Flanagan won three Olympic
medals (1900, 1904 and 1908), and was the apostle of the
'toe-turn'. He believed that by turning on the ball of the foot
and not letting the heel down at all, you could shorten the
turning axis and offer less resistance to the float of the
hammer. He managed to do four turns instead of the usual
three inside the seven-foot circle.

To do this while holding on to a steel ball on the end of a
piano wire, exerting a pulling force of many hundreds of
pounds, requires extraordinary precision. Later throwers
like Dr Pat O'Callaghan (Olympic champion in 1928 and
first man to throw further than 200 feet) were not pure
toe-turners: they started on the heel and went up on the toe.

This was despite the teaching of their coach, John Tallon,
who was a fanatical believer in the toe-turn. Tallon, who also
coached John Lawlor, is the mystery man of Irish athletics; to
this day no one can properly explain how a dapper little
Dublin tailor with no sports background came to know more
about the hammer than anybody in the world.

One day he waylaid Pat O'Callaghan outside the anatomy
room at the Royal College of Surgeons and declared that he
would make him the greatest hammer thrower in the world.
For some reason O'Callaghan, who had never met Tallon
before, was persuaded to accept him as his coach, and soon
had won his first Olympic championship. Later Tallon did

the same thing with Healion, who was also a student at the Royal College of Surgeons.

You could see Tallon on Sunday mornings scurrying through the city, barely reaching the elbows of the giants he coached and heading for some secret field where he had obtained permission for his throwers to plough up the turf with their ferocious missiles. While his pupils threw, he might shake his head dolefully as he peered down at their feet. If the heel went down, it was not a perfect throw for the maestro.

A strange thing, according to the late Bert Healion, is that Tallon's theory may have been the right one. Healion told me that although he himself used the toe-and-heel turn, he believed that the ultimate hammer throw would be made by an athlete who would be able to do four turns up on the toe.

Healion had miserable luck in his hammer career. He threw 204 ft 5 in before a committee of newsmen at a competition at the New York Athletic Club in 1948, becoming the first man to throw over 200 ft; but his record was not recognised as he had forfeited his amateur status by wrestling as a professional.

Pat O'Callaghan also became a professional wrestler in the United States for a while, and is reputed on one occasion to have gone into three hammer spins with his opponent at the other end of his arms. When he let go, the spectators had the awesome experience of seeing a seventeen-stone man flying like an astronaut through the smoke-filled auditorium.

O'Callaghan would almost certainly have won his third Olympic title in 1936 but for the fact that Irish athletes were suspended at the time and he had to watch from the stand as a German won the event.

At Belfield last Sunday, as the young athletes threw, there was an atmosphere of ritual. Very little talk considering there were twelve boys in the vicinity. Conway's curt commands were the only sounds to interrupt the zing of the hammer-wire and the swish of feet in the cement circle.

'Head up.'

'Too slow first turn!'

As the lads gather speed in the throw, you recognise that it is a battle about who will go out of the circle first – boy or hammer. The arc of the ball widens, the feet make twinkling turns so as to get the body ahead and fire the hammer instead of it firing them. Then the rapid whiplash which lifts the ball up and into the air.

As throw after throw is unleashed, you realise you have never seen so many hammers in the air before. The effect is psychedelic. Silver balls like circles of fire humming into the sun; young men striving to be gods, their hands stretched outwards towards the departing ball as it speeds towards the brazen clouds where, we are told, divinities rest.

29th June, 1975

An athletic Oblomov

The other day, a seventy-three-year old man ran a lap round the outside of the Olympic Stadium in Los Angeles. He hadn't been able to get in, as the building was locked on a public holiday. Forty-eight years before, Robert Morton Newburgh Tisdall won the Olympic 400 metres hurdles title there.

I caught hold of him recently on a visit to Ireland.

'It looks very nice to-day,' he says of his old home, Hazelpoint, at Nenagh, in Tipperary, which he is visiting from Australia via the United States: 'There are creepers growing on the walls. It has become quite venerable since I was there.'

Tisdall remains Ireland's only medallist in an Olympic hurdles event. He must have been the most under-trained athlete to win an Olympic gold medal since the First World War, a sort of athletic Oblomov who actually went to bed for a week before the Olympic competition, running exactly one lap before going on the track for the first heat.

'I was always afraid of going stale,' he explained. 'Most of my training was done at Ballybunion strand, and on a greyhound track nearby, where I was once most disheartened when the electric hare got going and left me nowhere.'

In fact, he competed in only three 400 metres hurdles races before he ran in the Olympics!

'But I was a natural. I held the 440 yards public schools' record, and I was also a high hurdler; put the two together and you should get a result.'

The result was that he beat Lord Burghley, the 1928 Olympic champion, and Morgan Taylor, the 1924 Olympic champion, as well as Glenn Hardin, the United States record-holder. He equalled the world record in the semi-finals, and broke it in the final with 51.8 sec. But it did not go into the record books because he knocked the last hurdle, a mishap which under the present rules would not have mattered.

In 1931, the year before the Los Angeles Olympics, Tisdall had become a household name. He won four events within two hours for Cambridge in the University match – the shot, the long jump, the high hurdles and the 440 yards. He could have won the 220 yards hurdles (at which he held the British record) as well, but generously gave his place to a team-mate who was in line for a Blue. The newspapers were full of him, because in addition to his all-round ability he had film-star good looks. Blue-eyed, black-haired, with the profile of a Phidias sculpture, he looked like a rather healthy version of Robert Taylor.

The future seemed secure after he took a degree at Cambridge:

'I chucked exercise for a while, and went off as ADC to the Maharajah of Baroda. I led rather a lotus life for about nine months, going around Europe, till I got the idea to try for the Olympics.'

When he did decide to have a go, Tisdall had to 'run three miles a few times a week just to get the feeling back in my legs'.

He was eligible to compete for Britain as well as Ireland. Had he gone to the Games on the British team, Tisdall could have had the world at his feet when he came back, a Cambridge man with an Olympic Gold. I asked him why he chose Ireland: 'My dear fellow, I'm an Irishman.'

So it was the Irish flag, only ten years old, that was raised when Tisdall stood on the victors' rostrum in Los Angeles. And instead of the British anthem it was *The Soldier's Song* which resounded across the stadium.

Tisdall had grown up on the banks of the lordly Shannon at Lough Derg. His father was an Anglo-Irish gentleman who sent him to Shrewsbury (where he won the public schools' gymnastics championship), and afterwards to university.

When Bob Tisdall had to make a choice between two ends of a hyphen, he opted for the Irish end, while retaining the best of good feelings with the other end:

'Later, during the Second War, when I was in South Africa, we formed the South African Irish Regiment. We'd seven MCs in it from the First War. We also had bagpipes and kilts and an Irish wolfhound. It was tremendous. We fought in the Western Desert campaign, and I finished up a major.'

After that it was Kenya, Rhodesia, Tanzania and Ireland for Tisdall, before he settled in Queensland. If he had not emigrated, his popularity could have made him a candidate for president of Ireland. He came from the ascendancy class but he had identified with the new state. With his looks, style and achievement, he seems the ideal modern Irishman. I remember a sports promoter from Nenagh telling me once how Tisdall had returned his expenses after a track meeting there because he didn't want to be compensated for coming back to his own town. Stories like this about Tisdall are legion.

To-day he believes Australia is the coming country. He is very fit, and ran in a four-mile race last year. He even jumped a high hurdle to show that his legs were still loose. On Lough Derg last week, he and his son won first prize in a yachting race on the lake where he had first competed sixty years ago.

Does he have plans for the future? 'Yes, I am saving up for the 1984 Olympic Games in Los Angeles.'

By then, the stadium won't be locked, and Bob Tisdall will be able to view the track where he ran himself into history on 1st August, 1932.

29th June, 1980

Just how hard is it to win an Olympic medal the hard way?

Claude Stevens who won the silver medal at the discus at the Montreal Disabled Athletes Olympics is totally paralysed from the chest down. At Montreal he threw the One Kilo Discus 75 feet. The difficulty about assessing paraplegic athletics is relating it to non-disabled athletic performances. Then I had a wheeze. I asked Phil Conway, the Irish shot putt record holder (60 ft 3½ in) and former Irish discus record holder (167 ft 7 in) and New England Collegiate champion, if he would get into a wheelchair and throw against Claude Stevens.

Conway agreed. The stipulation was that he was not to use his legs. He had to let them hang in the wheelchair so that he was roughly in the position of a man trying to throw something out of a children's swing. He had one advantage though over Stevens. He could twist his hips where a great deal of the impetus in the discus throw comes from. Stevens, on the other hand, is unable to achieve any movement at all in his body below the nipples of his chest. The judge was to be Michael Cunningham who had won the Gold Medal in the javelin at the Montreal Disabled Olympics.

The interesting thing about Stevens' preliminary swing was how closely it resembled the pose in the classical Greek sculpture, the Discobulus of Myron.

After he lowers his head Stevens lets his arm back in a swoop that waves up and down like a swan's wing coming off the water or Toscanini's baton at the commencement of Beethoven's Fifth, until travelling through a number of arcs the discus is finally launched into the air. Of three throws his best was 74 feet – only a few feet short of his Olympic throw. 'My day is made up,' he said with a pleased grin.

Phil Conway settled in the chair in obvious uneasiness. He is a keen competitor and he didn't want to lose. His first throw was behind Claude's, so was his second. But he managed to get 9 inches in front on his third throw. Result – Conway 73 feet, Stevens 72 feet 3 inches.

As a P.T. expert (he has a Master's degree from the University of Springfield, Massachusetts) Conway perceived the muscular advantage he had even without his legs being on the ground. 'I could feel my erector spinae tense up and give me a base to throw against. Something simply Claude hadn't got.'

Conway is thirty-two and one of the most perfect physical specimens in Ireland today with the tapered legs of a sprinter and the torso of a Mr World.

Stevens is fifty-seven though he looks about thirty-five. It was becoming paralysed in fact that turned him toward athletics. Up to that he had no interest in sport of any kind. He had been a merchant seaman for twenty years until he fell off the hold of a ship and became paralysed. After being hospitalised for nine years he had become almost a basket case. 'I was swathed in rugs. I couldn't hold my head up without a rest. I had no interest in life until (looking with a grin at two other wheelchair athletes) these bastards got at me to take up sport. I had never been near a sports field before that. I was literally an old man dribbling. Then my whole life changed.'

Looking at him it is hard to think of how he must have appeared to his companions four years ago when he came out of hospital. He is fit, bronzed, very good looking with a youthful appearance. His daily training schedules are ferocious. 'I do two hours weightlifting, one hour's push-ups, an hour's road work, that means going up and down roads on my wheelchair, and about an hour of warming up and actual discus throwing. I do this as well as some archery and putting the shot.'

Stevens maintains that the exercise affects his whole outlook. 'It makes you mentally alert, aware of things in an almost psychedelic way. The greatest cure for depression.'

Certainly, Claude and his other mates in their wheelchairs didn't seem depressed as we drove home. They were even telling jokes.

'There was this guy who flew to Lourdes for a cure but he was so jacked when he got there that they were afraid to take him out of his wheelchair for fear he'd collapse. So they put him, wheelchair and all, into the sacred pool.'

'Did it cure him?' I asked breathlessly.

'No, but when he came out the wheelchair had a new pair of tyres.'

17th July, 1977

Billy would've run a mile

It is sad to see these days only a few hundred attend athletic meetings at Santry Stadium. The trouble is that the man who created the venue is dead. If Billy Morton were alive the crowd would probably have overflowed into the nearby Dublin Airport. He was one of the great promoters of our time.

'If it rains next Monday, Billy will run a regatta,' someone said about him, referring to his extraordinary ability to draw the crowds.

If Billy Morton came into a room people turned round to look at him. He was a small man with silver hair and a massive, intriguing head. His eyes were twinkling Irish, but his nose gave him the look of a Roman Emperor whose ancestors had a predilection for Ruths amid the alien corn. He ran his meetings like Napoleon on the battlefield, walking up and down with the instructions pouring left and right out of his mouth.

Billy Morton had one central ambition – to build a cinder track in Ireland, where athletes up to then had competed on grass. Because he understood the word glamour better than anybody else in Ireland at that time, he used his genius for promotion to raise money to build the track.

The first thing was to get foreign athletes over to Dublin. Conditions were primitive in Ireland then. But post-war England was hungry and Ireland had the food. I can still see Morton at London's White City Stadium during some of the big meets after the war. He would be equipped like a Lipton salesman weighed down with a huge handbag full of eggs, bacon and butter, commodities almost impossible to buy at that time in post-war Britain.

There was a keen demand on British athletes then all over Europe and Billy knew he had to have something else besides to bag his prey. He would sit in dressing rooms after meetings displaying his goods.

'I don't know if I can make it, Billy.'

'How long is it since you have had a fresh egg?'

'Before the war.'

'Here's a dozen.'

With watering lips the athlete signed.

Billy had another tack for US athletes who had plenty of food. In their case, with real genealogical skill, he would pin down what part of Ireland their ancestors had come from. A trip was promised to the family homestead and they too were caught in the Morton net.

'Billy, both my parents were black.'

'You've red sideburns.'

'What the hell, Billy.'

'You must have had an Irish grandfather.'

The meetings were phenomenal. In 1950 he crammed 45,000 people into Lansdowne Road rugby ground. A massed choir sang the Hallelujah Chorus from Handel's *Messiah*. A flock of pigeons rose from the centre of the pitch. Billy's sardonic voice from the loudspeaker addressing the crowd was one of the events of the evening.

'Everyone down.'

Then.

'Can everyone see me?'

From the crowd: 'No.'

Then Billy would say, 'because if you can't I want you to come up to my shop on Monday so that I can fix you up with a pair of glasses.'

As he was an optician by profession, the Ophthalmic Association got a bit shirty about these goings-on till they realised Morton did it much more for the joke than for the advertising.

His luck was extraordinary. People began to talk about 'Morton weather'. Always the sun shone brilliantly for Billy's meetings.

He had had the same sort of luck when he was an athlete running in the Irish marathon championship in 1936. He was a few hundred yards behind the first runner when they had neared the finishing point at Croke Park Stadium. But the first man couldn't get into the grounds as the gate was locked.

As soon as Billy puffed up he quickly organised someone to open the gate and then beat his opponent in the race around the track to win an Irish marathon championship.

His belief in his own good fortune allowed him to wait patiently each time an Irish athletic star would lose form. This meant that the ingredient necessary for his monster meetings, the contest between a native champion and an international star, would be missing. But as one champion went another turned up.

His first crowd-puller was John Joe Barry, the 'Ballincurry hare', who was the only man in the world in 1949 to run three miles inside fourteen minutes, two miles inside nine minutes and one mile inside four minutes ten seconds. Then when Barry gave up, along came Ron Delany, whose series of battles with Brian Hewson were the fulfilment of Billy's dream.

'A good Irishman against a good Englishman in the mile and there's no stadium in Ireland big enough to hold the crowds.'

In the 'fifties Morton became a world figure in athletics. He even popped up behind the Iron Curtain from time to time. Most officials would keep mum in the Cold War atmosphere of the Eastern countries then. But Billy always seemed to be able to know the right thing to say.

Once after a meeting in Prague he stood up at a dinner which was attended by worker delegates from all over the state. He drew attention to the fact that no one so far had mentioned the men who swept and cleaned the stadium – the workers. He was immediately showered with roses by the delegates present and finished the night by doing an Irish jig and singing 'Father O'Flynn'.

When he landed in Tunisia on an athletics trip his first comment was: 'This is a very arable land.'

In 1958 he had saved enough money to get the stadium

under way. He had it built at Santry on the edge of the city. The place had an air of magic from the start. In July 1958 five men broke the world record for the mile at Santry Stadium. The next night the world's two- and three-mile records were broken. 'It's greater than Lourdes,' a spectator said to me as we filed out of the stadium after the second night.

The astonishing thing about Morton's achievement was that it was done as a part-time, unpaid job and that the people he worked for from the AAU of Ireland could have been of little help to him. Incredibly there were less than a dozen athletic clubs at that time who were affiliated to the International Amateur Athletic Association and who could compete at Billy's meetings.

The officials of these clubs were often clerks or Boys' Brigade officials, hardly the type to embark on Barnum and Bailey presentations of the sort that Billy sponsored. For many at that time the thought of a cinder track in Ireland was as remote as a pork factory in Israel.

But Billy bribed them too – made them time-keepers, judges and announcers, got them out in front of massive crowds so that in the office on Monday morning they had a new status as participants in the most glamorous event in Ireland at that time.

Five years ago Billy Morton fell down a hole in a Dublin street. It was an incongruous way for a man whom the gods smiled on to meet his death. For a long time many people couldn't believe that he was gone. He had seemed part of the personality of the city like Brendan Behan, Sean O'Casey or Barry Fitzgerald. A light had gone out that had lit the place for two decades.

A week before his death I had received a prize from him as a member of an Old Ireland team which had played Old England at soccer at Dalymount Park. It had been a typical Morton promotion.

A record crowd, an electric atmosphere and Stanley Matthews. When Billy came to present his prize to the last player (who was bald) I knew there was a crack coming. He looked around with mischievous eyes the way he would before saying anything funny, drawing listeners into his orbit. 'Eh, Hair oil – here's yours,' he said. The timing was perfect; and the crowd chortled.

Billy once told Brendan O'Reilly (the former Irish record holder in the high jump) when they met in the US that he knew 'he belonged to the best little country in the world, but if he had the population of the US to tap, he could really have done something big'. There was no doubt he could have. He was one of the great promoters of his age. He never took a penny for his work. It's sad that last week there should only be a few hundred people at the Morton Mile.

Billy wouldn't have given a damn though. He'd have known something was bound to turn up.

27th July, 1975

RUGBY

Spreading the gospel of rugby

He has been banned from French television as a commentator because the authorities consider that his opinions are too abrasive, but he loves rugby so much that it will not stop him watching every match he can. The unusual thing about this commentator, Henri Pistre, is that he is a village priest seventy-four years old. He became a nationally-known rugby writer years ago when he wrote a column for a little paper in the South-West, *Courier Sportif du Tarn*. His comments were quoted by rugby fans throughout France.

About one referee, the Abbé Pistre said (after accusing the unfortunate man of imbibing too liberally before the match):

'His perfumed luggage included a tiny hunting horn instead of a whistle, but did not include a lorgnette indispensable to someone so short-sighted.'

About another writer who criticised what the Abbé considered a good match, he wrote:

'He has a refrigerator where his heart should be.'

And writing for *Midi-Libre* in 1960 about the France–England match in Paris – an affair notable for repeated scrummages – he said:

'We don't go to see systematic burial at a rugby match. What are funeral undertakers for?'

Such remarks spring not from anger, but from the Abbé's love of rugby, the ruling passion of his life. On the day he was ordained in 1921, the Bishop remarked that Father Pistre looked bulkier than usual. The young priest opened the top of his soutane, and displayed underneath the jersey of his

27

rugby club, Albi, which he had worn throughout the cere-mony.

The trouble about Henri Pistre's rugby career was that those who controlled French clerical teaching at that time, considered the male leg indecent. Poor old Henri and his school friends at the seminary had to play games in their soutanes in case the exposure of their knees might excite other seminarians. In fact, he had high-jumped 5 ft 5 in incommoded by what amounts to a full-length black serge garment.

National service was Henri's liberation. His officers had no such reservations about baring the male knee. And when Henri Pistre showed he could do 100 yards in 10 seconds, he was quickly put by his colonel into the regimental rugby team.

In three weeks, Albi, one of the great French First Division sides, had grabbed him. He would almost certainly have been a French international (three of the side, Vaysse, Gomet and Marcet were in the French team), but when his military service ended, he returned to his seminary.

'God won, but only just. Luckily he is not jealous,' Henri Pistre says now.

As a young priest he began his second career as a rugby writer. First he wrote anonymously under the name of 'The Grumbler'. When people began to wonder who the interest-ing commentator was, Father Pistre, to put them off the scent, invented a wife for himself. He began to write about going to the match 'with my wife Virginia' and would relate her comments on the game. Later he dropped his pseudonym, and to-day writes a much-read weekly column for *Midi-Libre*.

Though he will not be on television this year, the Abbé Pistre still loves rugby passionately. I went to see him last week at his parish in Noailhac, near Castres in the South-West. It is a village of 400 people. The Abbé lives in a typical parish priest's house that might have come out of a novel by Georges Bernanos.

He was saying Mass in the open air when I arrived. It was All Saints Day. For a wild moment I thought the angelic altar boys in their white surplices were singing a rugby song. But it turned out that one of the best-known French hymns is written to the tune of *Auld Lang Syne*. Then there was a baptism. I listened to the Abbé's words. I wondered whether he would deliver one of his well known benedictions: 'May the good God make you strong, and don't muff your drop goals' but I wasn't near enough to hear properly.

We went to the Abbé's house. His drawing room has the frugal furniture of village priests everywhere. There was the bookcase, the religious statue. The only modern thing was an enormous colour television in the centre for watching le rugby.

The Abbé Pistre has a splendid head, a chiselled peasant face straight out of a Millet painting. He talks about rugby in a lyrical way, but has the analytical approach of the French. How could a Frenchman have acquired such a love of an English game, I asked?

'Art has no native country.'

'But is rugby, Monsieur l'Abbé, an art form?'

'You must think of rugby as an art form, otherwise it becomes a battle of thugs.'

I asked him if a man of his personality and ability might not have become a bishop had it not been for his dedication to sport.

'Why should I need to be a bishop? I am already a Pope.'

That is in fact how he is known in the South-West – the Pope of Rugby. When a local wine millionaire took the Abbé to Rome, the old man remarked on his return:

'It was a summit meeting – two Popes.'

To understand how the Abbé can say such things without irreverence, one must know the sporting atmosphere of the South-West. It is the rugby capital of France, if not of the world. In the cities and towns people eat, drink and sleep rugby: Tarbes, Béziers, Lourdes (Jean Prat), Mazamet (Lucien Mias), Mont-de Marsan (the Boniface brothers), these are world names in the game. When the Abbé declared a while ago in his weekly column that Béziers would win the French championship for the next five years, no one was surprised when it turned out that way: 'Isn't the Pope infallible!'

A long-haired hippy went to him recently:

'Monsieur l'Abbé will you do me a favour? I met an Irish girl at the France–Ireland international who was shouting so much that I gave her a drink. Now we are getting married. I want to have it done by the Pope of Rugby.'

The Abbé Pistre is not in the least disturbed by his dismissal from French television:

'After all, I do not comment to amuse the mob. I am not in the least bit bitter about it. They have come to me. I have never asked to go to them.'

After his television performances, he was flooded with correspondence, most of it complimentary, some not. Young girls wrote to him begging him to forward the addresses of muscular rugby players. He dealt with his Press like any pop star.

Yet the Abbé does not seem to have been affected by his fame. When he talks about his parish work, it is clear that this is the centre of his life. He always dresses in his parish priest's gear – soutane and wide-brimmed hat – and is very much against the mod dress worn by young clergymen to-day. He remains the Curé de Campagne, still with his two loves, 'le rugby et le Bon Dieu'.

9th November, 1975

Rugby's ruthless element

If Billy Beaumont continued playing rugby, his doctors told him he would run the risk of becoming paralysed on one side. The English captain was lucky to find out in time. Other players have not been so fortunate. Since 1976 there have been six Irish players paralysed from the neck down as a result of rugby injuries. They have no sensation below the level of the neck, no control over bladder or bowel functions, nor can they experience sexual feelings. One of them, Fergus Barrett, lives in a respirator which inflates and deflates his lungs by artificial means. Five out of six of these injuries occurred in scrummages or loose rucks. Since there have been no recorded cases of quadraplegia at the National Rehabilitation Institution at Dun Laoghaire resulting from rugby injuries before 1976 it is not unreasonable to conclude that there is a new element in rugby which was not there before.

Dr Gregg, Head of the Rehabilitation Institution, described to me how a neck injury can occur in the scrum.

'If the scrum collapses the fellow opposite you brings your head down. If it's in a vulnerable position your neck breaks with a crack which can be heard. If the spinal cord is severed, as in the case of a quadraplegic, there is no further transmission of nerve impulses nor can there be at any time in the future.'

Dr Gregg points out that the same thing can happen in a loose ruck, especially when an extra player adds his weight to the maul. As a result of this horrifying increase in serious injuries, is there not a case for the radical alteration in the rules for loose rucks or even abolishing the scrum altogether?

Football games which have no scrums have a demonstrably better record. For instance, Gaelic football is played by 200,000 footballers in Ireland. It is a tough, physical game but there is nothing resembling a scrum in it. There have been no recorded cases of quadraplegia resulting from injuries in Gaelic Football.

It is harder to think of a tougher game than Rugby League, yet there has only been one Rugby League quadraplegic in a decade and that was caused by a rare sandwich tackle. There are many more Rugby League players in Britain than there are Rugby Union players in Eire, 17,000 as opposed to 10,000.

One difference between the two games is that loose rucks don't occur in Rugby League. Also the League scrum is a totally different animal from the Rugby Union one. A spectator watching a Rugby League scrum could be forgiven for thinking that the players are at times merely lying against one another. I asked a former Rugby League international about this.

'In League it's much more a case of leverage than pushing. The scrummage laws are quite different, even the way the scrum half puts the ball into the scrum. Besides, there are only six forwards to Rugby Union's eight.'

Before the War, for instance, it would have been unthinkable for forwards to run full tilt into mauls as they do now, or leap into mauls with the knee up. These days front rows face each other like Andalusian bulls ready to snap their necks into place. Charging is illegal, but if one is to judge by current practice this is not an easy rule to enforce.

Why has there been, then, such a dramatic increase in quadraplegic injuries since 1976? One answer is that the nature of the game has changed. Rugby was originally a game where the restraints of good form restricted dangerous play. But that has changed. The desire to win has overridden the concept that the game should be played for its own sake. Dr Gregg agrees that there has been a change of some kind and maintains that 'a ruthless element has come into the game'.

Rugby Union legislators are notoriously conservative and

dislike changes in the rules, especially if it appears that they are following Rugby League precedents. But it is essential that they face up to the medical evidence available. If they are convinced that something should be done they should give serious attention to revising the scrummage laws.

The President of the Leinster Branch of the Irish Rugby Football Union is by no means untypical in his attitude. In an interview in the *Irish Times* in December 1981 he said that the most recent reports issued by the Irish Rugby Football Union indicated that the incidence of serious injury 'is relatively low'. He then went on to say that if young boys do not join clubs and participate in sport they will turn to drugs.

'I see them on the golf course; nice well-mannered young fellows looking for mushrooms to sniff. My son could be among them and I am happy to know that he is playing rugby down at Blackrock.'

A substantial section of rugby's legislators are distancing themselves from the available facts because possibly they feel the game is under threat; but it is surely consistent to love rugby and at the same time seek to remove obvious dangers that have crept into it. The tragedy of the quadraplegics and the implications of Billy Beaumont's retirement should not be pushed under the carpet just to smooth some people's ruffled feelings.

14th February, 1982

Jack Kyle at 50

Even legends grow old. Jack Kyle hasn't. He's back from Zambia this summer and looks the same as when I first saw him twenty-five years ago; wavy brown hair, clear skin, shy smile. What I have always wanted to know was how Kyle did it. He went past opponents in a way that no ball player in these islands has ever done. Stanley Matthews used a body swerve of 45 degrees that sent you yards in the opposite direction to which he was going; Lewis Jones jinked, stopped, and started again like a dodgem car; Richard Sharpe used a combination of dummy and swerve. But Kyle simply ran through without any artifice.

Now at lunch in Belfast I could ask him. But he barely remembers his famous tries. 'I wasn't even a sprinter at school,' he says somewhat apologetically.

He went past his opponents on instinct. For instance, he got a try in the first Test at Auckland in 1950 against New Zealand which is regarded by many there as the greatest ever seen. Kyle's only memory of the try is something vague about 'cutting inside Bob Scott at full-back after a set scrum'.

In fact, the ball didn't come to Kyle at all from his own scrum. Quite the opposite. George Norton, the Bective, Ireland and Lion full-back, who was at the match fortunately has an almost video tape memory and was able to give this description of Kyle's astonishing run:

'New Zealand got the ball on the half-way and the fly-half kicked ahead. Kyle jumped and got it in the air with his hand over his head. He began from a standing start. You know the way he went biz-z-z like a motor cycle starting up. He beat the out-half and inside-centre who were coming at him. He was now down at the '25' with Bob Scott the full-back coming at him from one side and Charington, the New Zealand wing, a hefty Maori character, coming at him from the other. Somehow or other Kyle gave Scott the idea that he was going outside him but instead went inside against all the rules and succeeded in also beating Charington, who should have been able to sandwich him with Scott. Charington chased him and caught him by the collar as he reached the line, but Jack shook himself off like a terrier and scored.'

After the match an old Maori asked to be shown into the dressing-room. There were tears in his eyes. 'You're greater than Cookie,' he said to Kyle. (Bert Cook was the legendary All Black fly-half of the twenties.)

There was a similar Kyle try in 1948 in the Scottish match in Dublin. Karl Mullen got a lovely heel for Ireland outside the Scottish '25'. Almost as the ball left the scrum-half's hands to go into the scrum, Kyle's feet twinkled into top speed. He took a crisp pass from Hugh DeLacy and ran their between the fly-half and centre to place the ball under the post. There wasn't an iota of a swerve or jink. The Scottish line was still in perfect formation, not having moved from their positions when Kyle had reached the post.

How were these runs done? There is no adequate explanation. It was as if Kyle had a built-in computer which estimated for him to the last centimetre just how many yards he had to travel to beat an opponent. As players converged on him the computer engaged in numerous permutations before he made his decision to shift himself to a certain spot. All this, of course, took place in a fraction of a second, but then that is the way one is led to believe computers operate.

Kyle didn't just rely on his instinctive gift. He was a demon for hard work.

'When I was at Queens, Belfast,' he says, 'Ernie Strathdee and myself used to go out to Jack McDowell who had invented a machine that sent the ball back as if it was a scrum.'

For hours, as the machine disgorged footballs, Kyle would luxuriate in a spray of passes hurled out by Strathdee.

He wasn't a natural kicker with both feet. But after a year or two in first-class rugby, he kicked as well with his right as his left, a low hard unspinning punt that squeezed every inch out of the sideline.

He was, however, weak in one department.

'I was a bad passer of the ball. I didn't know this until I saw myself on film. Then it was too late to change.'

Kyle could be called the Marcus Aurelius of rugby, a stoic who would wait months for an opening without being tempted to probe for ones that weren't there. Then when it came – whoosh, he was gone. Because of his waiting tactics he developed a defensive technique that has never been mastered by any other fly-half. He used to run behind his backs like a No 8 does to-day, and frequently cut off a wing going for the line. Once against England there were two white jerseyed players with nothing between them and a certain try. Only Kyle could have done it. He swooped from nowhere and tackled both of them – knocking one into the other.

Kyle had a remarkable head-master at Belfast Royal Academy. This was Alec Foster, an ex-rugby international, who had a massive repertoire of Irish ballads, which he would sing on football occasions. Foster kindled in Kyle a love of Irish culture, a rare enough occurrence among rugby-playing Belfast boys.

'He used to give me books like *The Fair Hills of Ireland* to read so that I understood what was around me much better when I went South. I don't think I ever enjoyed touring anywhere like I did there, especially Galway. It meant everything to me that we represented. Then, when I went South, I understood the whole of Ireland, because it showed that Irishmen can get together.'

Why then did he leave and go to Indonesia and Zambia? Kyle is reticent about this. There may be a clue in a remarkable letter he sent to the *Irish Times* in 1967 – well before the bloodshed in Ulster began. The letter was addressed to the Reverend Ian Paisley for his 'obsessive ravings'. In it Kyle accused Paisley of 'sowing seeds that create evil from which springs despicable actions'.

It may be that Kyle chose to work in underdeveloped countries, because as an admirer of Albert Schweitzer he felt that he should put the success he could enjoy at home at the service of less fortunate people. But it was from Africa that he would glimpse the dark among his own.

Nowadays he is the ideal of a rounded Irishman. He will quote Yeats (lovingly), Edmund Burke or Synge to illustrate a point. He is a successful surgeon. He has that serenity which can go with those who are gifted supremely, and who never had to engage in the hard, horrible struggle against anonymity.

Even when in the season before the 1950 New Zealand tour, Kyle seemed to have lost form and the duffle coats were muttering through their purple lips into their whiskey that he was finished, he just sailed along and didn't give a damn.

At fifty – still a cool guy.

12th October, 1975

Jammie Clinch – a living legend

Jammie Clinch was bitten in the arm by Wavell Wakefield (now Lord Wakefield) in the 1924 Ireland *v* England match. When 'Wakers' took his fangs out, Jammie just grinned at him. He had been holding him and the ball in a stranglehold and he knew his opponent required to breathe.

'Rugby is a rough game,' Jammie explains, 'and if you don't play it extremely robustly, stay at home.'

When he was eight years old, his father told him:

'Put the fellow two feet into the ground when you tackle him.'

Jammie, with thirty caps between 1923 and 1930, was one of the toughest players in the history of the game. At fifteen stone and 6 ft 2 in, there wasn't an ounce of fat on him. Players got hurt just bouncing off him. Once he and Tom Blakiston were found by Tommy Vile, the referee, scrapping away for the ball. When he turned them over, Vile saw they were both laughing.

'That was the spirit in those days. It was rough, but definitely not dirty. You never went out on the field to get anyone, like you hear them talking about in the pavilions these days.'

Jammie has firm views on the punching affair that took place on the field at this month's Colours Match at Lansdowne Road.

'If I had been the referee, I would have put the ball under my arm and walked off and said, "Look here, lads, you don't need me".'

As I was meeting Jammie on the day of the Oxford and

Cambridge match, I thought it might be fun to watch it on television with him. After there had been five consecutive scrums with only a minute or two between them, he commented, 'Now they'll have a committee meeting. All they need is an Archbishop to bless the ball.'

The hooker poised in statuesque pose for thirty seconds before throwing in the ball brought this comment:

'He is saying PRQ 234, which means the bus goes to Ballybough.'

When the front row forward shoved his way over for an Oxford try, Jammie said:

'There was no point in tackling him. I would have reefed the ball out of his hands. Bloody marvellous, isn't it? The first try Oxford have got in four years. I thought the object of this game was to cross the line.'

About a player who seemed to be constantly on the ground:

'There's nothing wrong with him that a good vasectomy wouldn't cure.'

I was sitting beside a legend. I had grown up with tales of Jammie Clinch. Every rugby book you read had a Clinch story or two in it. He has that sort of face which makes you laugh before he opens his mouth. He speaks in that delightful Dublin Protestant drawl that Shaw and Yeats used to charm the English. Jammie sharpened his mind as a student in the Bailey, drinking with what was probably one of the wittiest groups in these islands, Oliver St John Gogarty, James Stephens, Arthur Griffith.

A good Bailey tale concerned Jammie's reply to an American lady who spoke to him while he was sitting on the rails outside Trinity.

'It's a big place,' she said. 'I've been three hours going through it.'

'Ma'am,' Jammie replied. 'I have been here seven years and I am not through it yet.'

He left his medical studies for a while and joined the Middlesex Regiment. That got him to Shanghai for some fighting. Presently he won a Sweep there and went on a world tour. Afterwards he came back to Ireland to resume his medical studies at the Royal College of Surgeons. Long before this he had fulfilled his life's ambition which was to play for Ireland.

Rugby had been part of his existence since he could talk. His father, Dr A. D. Clinch, also an international, used to say:

'I didn't send my son to Trinity to get a degree. He was sent there to play for Ireland.'

When Jammie and his brother were six years of age, his father gave Jammie a football boot for his left foot and the brother one for his right. This was intended to make them kick with the foot they weren't used to.

'It was a magnificent notion,' Jammie comments, 'except we simply swapped boots as soon as he was out of sight.'

The most important influence on Jammie's rugby career was the Rev C. V. Rooke, the Irish international forward who is generally credited with laying the foundations for modern back row forward play.

'My father got Rooke to teach us. He could do anything with the ball. Even the way he held it showed he had a feeling for it. He could catch it with his fingertips and pass as well as Adrian Stoop. He had a marvellous kick with both feet. I determined to be like him. When I went to Trinity I learned a lot from Jack van Druten, the Springbok who was on the First Fifteen and was good in any department.'

This was the beginning of Jammie's phenomenal career in Irish rugby. He could kick with both feet better than most full backs. He covered behind his backs to bring off bone-shaking tactics like the one on Cove Smith at the corner flag at Twickenham in 1925, or to collect balls that had been dropped by the centres.

'I never scored because I always felt a back could do it better. In those days you must remember if you gave a second row forward a pass he didn't speak to you for a month.'

His wit on and off the field made him a legend. 'Oh, if only I had a bicycle,' he said in an aside to spectators as he headed for the line, ashen-faced and with his white headband, at Twickenham.

On another occasion, playing for A. T. Young's team out of position on the wing, he was thanked at the dinner afterwards by the opposition for winning the game for them.

'Ian Smith may be known as the "Flying Scotsman",' Jammie replied, 'but at home in Ireland I am known as the *Irish Mail* and I can assure you I am slightly faster than the Irish Female.'

Jammie has strong views on the modern game.

'There are far too many rules. As soon as anything goes wrong in the game, they make a new rule. It is just the same with government. Westminster is sinking two inches each year with the weight of Statute Books.'

He thinks the awful mess of modern scrummages could be solved by going back to an old rule.

'The ball should be put in as soon as three players are up. That's a scrum. They just step over it and you have the ball. It means of course that whoever gets up first must form the front row.'

He takes a dim view of players who try to build their strength up with special food.

'It has been reliably demonstrated that if you eat the cardboard box that holds most cereals, you get as much nourishment as from the food inside.'

Jammie belongs to a breed outworn. They believed in honour on the field and that you kept your word off it. If someone tackled you, you were able to take care of yourself. His sister who is a nun, aged seventy-eight, had just been attacked the day I met him by thugs who had tried to steal her car. She told Jammie she had hit one of the thieves with her elbow. When he asked her where she hit him, she replied that she hoped she had got him in the eye.

When Sister Gabriel got back to her convent, the Reverend Mother didn't seem surprised at her escape.

It was, she said, the least she'd expect from a sister of Jammie Clinch.

1st January, 1978

Kicking a way into literature

When I read that two Irish players had been suspended by the Irish Rugby Football Union after the recent France–Ireland B match, I thought how much better they ordered these things in the past.

In 1923, during the Ireland–France match at Colombes, Paris, Dick Collopy, an Irish forward, received a hefty boot in the mouth from a French player. The Frenchman was ordered off by an indignant referee; Dick's brother, Billy, pleaded for the Frenchman to be allowed back on the field.

This was done amid appreciative shouts of 'Les sportifs Irlandais' from the crowd. Before the end of the match the French player had left not only the field but the stadium – in an ambulance.

This match and the name Collopy became important to me because through them I was enabled to unravel a little of the most complicated work of modern literature, *Finnegans Wake* by James Joyce, which continues to confound critics.

One day in the Dublin Law Library an elderly barrister, William Fallon, hearing that I was a Joycean, came over to me to tell me that during the 1920s James Joyce had sent him occasional extracts from *Finnegans Wake*. This puzzled him because, though he had been at school with Joyce, he had not been able to understand why a world-famous writer should have sent him extracts from what was generally recognised as an incomprehensible book.

He showed me the extracts which had been published in *Transition*, a Paris avant-garde magazine. There was nothing in them as far as I could see which could give me a clue as to the reason for Joyce's gift.

I asked Fallon had he met Joyce in Paris at all before the material started to come in the post. Yes, he had. He had gone over to Paris for the French–Irish match in 1923 as a representative of the Irish Rugby Football Union. Naturally when he was there, he looked up his old school pal, who was now world-famous and whose recent novel *Ulysses* had had the distinction of being banned for obscenity in almost every country in the world.

'Joyce asked me what did I think of the match. I said I thought it was a good game; but I was surprised to learn that he had been at it. He never played rugby at school; he used to kick a ball like a girl, with the heel of his foot. When I told him I was surprised, he said: "I had to go to see the lads in green jerseys".'

With this information I went over the copies of *Transition* again. I knew Joyce, who conceived *Finnegans Wake* as a dream sequence, had a habit of sticking into it anything that came into his mind on the grounds that 'it happened'.

Then on one of the pages I spotted the magic word 'Collopy'. I checked on the rugby records. Two Collopy brothers had indeed been playing for Ireland in January, 1923, in Paris. The sentence in Joyce's chapter was 'By the horn of twenty, of both the two Saint Collopy's blackmail him I will.'

Was this enough? After all there were other Collopys in Ireland besides the rugby internationals.

But elsewhere in the chapter I found this: 'And I'll tell you the Bectives wouldn't hold me.'

Bective Rangers had been the club the Collopy brothers played for. On another page I found: 'In that united IRU stade'; surely an obvious reference to the Irish Rugby Union and the Stade Colombes.

Then there was a sequence of rugby metaphors to show the direction of Joyce's mind.

'I'd followed through my upfielded newviewscope the rugby moon cumuliously godrolling himself westasleep amuckst the cloud-scrums.'

The old maestro had been at his trick of sticking into the

text, as if he was making a plum pudding, whatever was available on the day he was at work.

But how, I wonder, are the critics of East Jesus, Kansas, to know who the 'Saint Collopys' were, apart from the fact that the brothers were anything but saints on the rugby field?

Why, above all, had he not explained to Fallon the reason he was sending the *Finnegans Wake* extracts to him?

Ten years after the match when Fallon went to Paris again, Joyce was able to remember the names of the 1923 side from start to finish and the clubs of the players. But he never referred to *Finnegans Wake*.

What if Joyce had played rugby? *Finnegans Wake* could have turned into a jig-saw of oval-ball references. You might not have been able to get into the Lansdowne bar on international day for the thesis hunters at your elbow with their pens poised.

As for the two Collopys, I feel they would have been amused by Joyce's stunt. A bit bemused perhaps by the referee, Alan Welsby, who sent the two players off in the B international. One thing about the '"Saint" Collopys'. They knew how to handle things when it turned rough.

28th December, 1975

'Cannonball Kevin' – the sporting doctor

If the International Olympic Committee really does convene in Moscow next summer one of those present will be a man who won full international caps at rugby and soccer – one of only two in the world to do so. Dr Kevin O'Flanagan, the Irish IOC representative, played rugby for Ireland against Australia in 1948, soccer for the Republic in the thirties and forties and even soccer for Northern Ireland in Victory Internationals. In war-time Dublin, his soccer exploits with Bohemians were sung about by kids in the streets:

'O'Flanagan, O'Flanagan,
There's that Bohemian man again
The fulls and halves you hear them cry
As he like lightning flashes by,
O'Flanagan, O'Flanagan
You can hear the goalie shout
Oh stop that man O'Flanagan
His shots I can't keep out.'

In 1946 he really hit world headlines when he turned out for the Arsenal in the English First Division. The idea of a doctor working all the week in a clinic and playing as an amateur with the professionals on a Saturday, caught the public imagination. The 'Flying Doc' was a real crowd-puller of an outside-left who shot on the run with either foot. A burst on the outside, and from 30 yards the goal would be in danger from a shot that made an 'oomph' sound as his boot connected. He got five goals against Plymouth Argyle, and against Bolton, he performed a feat which led George Allison, famous manager of Arsenal, to suggest that O'Flanagan was the hardest kicker of the dead ball he had ever seen. The *Daily Sketch* described it thus: 'Before he was ready to carry out his elaborately advertised intention of trying an impossible direct free-kick from 35 yards, Dr O'Flanagan carefully wiped the mud off the wet ball, and did everything except chalk his cue. It scraped the underside of the bar as it whipped through.'

He became known as 'Cannonball Kevin', and the crowds poured in. There were 62,000 inside Highbury, and 8,000 locked out, when Arsenal met Stoke City, who had had six successive wins and had just dropped Stanley Matthews. The Doc got the only goal of the match by beating McCue and Brigham, cutting into the centre and shooting with his right foot.

The extraordinary thing is that O'Flanagan didn't clock in for training at Highbury. 'I hadn't the time,' he told me. 'I was working with Dr Bill Tucker at Grosvenor Square, and I was determined to get on in my profession. That came first.'

He stayed with the Arsenal for two years, till he broke a wrist and was out of action for six months.

He was not only a footballer in both codes. With almost no training by modern standards, he twice won the Irish 100 yards championship in 10.1 sec. The national long jump title came his way twice, too, on the first occasion with a leap of 22 ft 10½ in.

The Doc is now sixty-one, but looks about forty-five, still with wavy black hair that made him known to football fans four decades ago. He plays golf off a six handicap, having taken up the game after he had finished with the others, but was soon down to two, good enough to beat, on one occasion, the Irish close champion.

When Kevin O'Flanagan's name comes up in Irish rugby circles, one game is always mentioned – the Blackrock *v* University College, Dublin, cup semi-final of 1945. Playing for University College, Dublin, O'Flanagan got the ball from the kick-off on the left wing in his own '25'. Then something happened that I have never seen before or since on a rugby field. He started to run diagonally across in the direction of the score-line, beating player after player. Several times he seemed to have been stopped, but on each occasion he was off with extraordinary acceleration to the next player, whom he would beat with a side-step or swerve. Some of his opponents actually had two goes at him. He seemed untackleable. He wasn't running through gaps. He was running at players and beating them. About two yards from the line, he handed the ball to the wing, who scored.

Kevin O'Flanagan never had to be taught to side-step or swerve. He went to a school, Synge Street, where they didn't play rugby or soccer. His skill on the football field came naturally to him. It was no wonder, then, that Tom Whittaker, Allison's successor at the Arsenal, said after he had seen O'Flanagan that if he could have got him to train 'he would have been one of the greatest players in football history'.

Kevin feels that English First Division football forty years ago was a faster game.

'I think a lot of this has to do with the time the modern goalkeeper spends with the ball. It slows down the game. They sometimes hold it for 30 seconds.'

He thinks there is too much passing back today:

'Arsenal's idea was to keep the ball out of your own half with a long ball to the wings and across, like Bobby Charlton used to do.'

It is difficult to get him to talk about the legends that have grown up about his feats on the field. Recently I heard a fellow swear that he'd seen the Doc break the net with a shot in Cork. But Kevin says he can't remember doing it. He does admit, though, that this story about his expenses at the Arsenal is true:

After his first match there, they asked him what his travelling expenses were. 'Fourpence' he replied. They thought he meant £40. But he didn't. He had got to Highbury by Tube, and that was the fare. Once, when he found money in his boot, he went to lost property in Highbury so that it could be returned to the rightful owner.

Kevin O'Flanagan was perhaps the last Corinthian. He could stay at the top with the pros without training, and didn't need time off from work to remain in world class. By the way, the only other man to be capped at full international level at rugby and soccer is Michael O'Flanagan. The name is no coincidence. He's Kevin's brother.

27th January, 1980

Rugby's Svengali

It had been a legend when you were growing up. Mark Sugden, Ireland's most capped scrum half, they told you, didn't just fool his opponents when he sold the dummy, he took in the spectators as well. Everyone in the stand thought he'd given the ball away till they noticed him sprinting away with it still in his hands. One player was so taken in by the beautifully executed dummy that he dived over the line without the ball. Eugene Davy who played as outhalf to Sugden, remembers:

'You almost thought the ball was in flight, that it had left his finger tips.'

And Morgan Crowe, the Irish centre threequarter, 1929–34, says:

'The dummy was so perfect you'd think you had the ball in your hands yourself.'

No player since has exploited the dummy as Sugden did. I went down to see him in Dartmouth where he lives to-day to ask him how it was done.

Mark is seventy-nine this year but looks in his sixties. He is 5 ft 11 in tall and has big feet. Was it my imagination about those flared nostrils and dark eyes? One thought of the DuMaurier drawings of Svengali who could make people do as he wished.

'I used to maintain the dummy was hypnotic,' Mark said, 'you did it with your eyes. First you gave the chap you were selling it to a lot of time to see it coming. You didn't look at him but at your own player who was to receive the ball. You should look into his eyes appealingly as if to say, for instance, if it was Denis Cussen, "here you are Denis, take it". If you convinced him he was getting it he would affect the fellow who was going to tackle you.'

I felt like stout Cortez gazing at the Pacific, on the threshold of discovery. Breathless, I asked what were the mechanics.

'It must be a slow movement. Slow and careful. You should hold the ball out before you bring it back and not snatch it quickly. I used to bend my far knee as I let my arms out to give the impression that I really was letting it go. I have, as you see, very long arms and you know, that helped.'

There was a famous occasion at Lansdowne Road in 1926 when Ireland beat England for the first time for fifteen years and Mark sent Denis Cussen through twice on the blind side with dummies.

'Well, they all seemed to work splendidly and of course if you got it to Denis at all he never thought of anything except going for the line like billyo. He ran 9.8 on grass for the 100 yards, the Irish record.'

Then there was the occasion in 1929, the first time Ireland beat England at Twickenham when Mark got the winning try after selling a barrage of dummies. Some maintain it was as many as four.

'Well, it was the greatest fun because for the first time we beat England and of course they were watching Denis that day and I got in myself.'

How did his opponents feel about all this?

'I remember Joe Periton the English wing forward. He was told beforehand to kick me in the teeth and pay no attention to any dummies I offered him. Well, I gave old Joe one and he tore off to squash Denis and there was no ball. He was dropped after that. Then there was Douglas Crichton-Miller (later Headmaster of Stowe) who was told to give me a damn good hiding and I sold him a few and he was dropped. I was sorry because they were awfully nice chaps.'

Understandably there were a number of players who were out to rough Mark up, but he had a protector.

'Jammie Clinch. He used to look after me. He'd say "who did that, I'll make an orange out of him".'

The astonishing thing is that Mark Sugden didn't play scrum half till his second year in Trinity College, Dublin. He had actually played centre for Leinster and one day was playing fly half for his university when Harry Thrift, the former Irish international and Trinity selector, came up to him and said:

'Sugden you're the worst fly half I've ever seen. Why don't you take up snooker?'

The result was that Mark tried scrum half and entered into football legend. He wasn't fast, and for the last five years of his international career he had no match practice.

'I was teaching in Glenalmond and I couldn't get away to play club football. I used to arrive in Dublin on Friday and have my first match of the year in Lansdowne Road in an international. I was as fresh as a daisy while the others were all suffering from bad ankles and things. I gave up smoking for the week before an international, but I always smoked one at lunch on the day of the match.'

The other remarkable thing about Mark Sugden is that he hasn't a drop of Irish blood in him. His father came from a family of Staffordshire architects and retired to Dublin where Mark grew up, and his mother was a Londoner.

'But I feel Irish, though I've lived in Dartmouth for a long time now.'

As I talked to him, indeed, his voice had begun to lapse into the Dublin drawl of which Jammie Clinch was a supreme exponent. At Trinity Mark was on the famous Trinity side which won the Leinster Cup for six years and which included as well as Jammie Clinch, Terence Millin and Victor Pike, Jack Van Druten, the legendary South African back row forward.

In summer he played golf and went to the dansants in Foxrock, where he lived near Sam Beckett, the writer, who was on the Trinity cricket team with him. After leaving Glenalmond Mark came to the Royal Naval College at Dartmouth where he taught modern languages and retired as Head of the Department there in 1974.

Today Mark lives a few hundred yards away from the College with his wife Hilda, plays golf and walks three miles a day. He once made 98 for Ireland against Essex and has been

Devon squash champion. As I said goodbye to him at Totnes Station I felt elated. A legend had played itself out in front of me: I had met the Svengali of the rugby field.

29th November, 1981

BOXING

Ali . . . poet with a punch-line

I was coming back from Chicago after a television show. As I got on the plane I saw a man through the glass panel of the first-class cabin. It was like someone I'd seen twenty years ago – the young Cassius Clay. It couldn't be, but it was – the butterfly himself.

''Lo,' said Muhammad Ali.

'Hello,' I said.

'This is a poet,' he explained to his travelling companion, a black gentleman with a broken nose.

Ali said he'd come down to my seat in a while. I was surprised when he did, 15 minutes later. He wanted to talk 'poetry'. I showed him a book of my poems. He inspected it with care, placing an enormous thumb and finger on the pages to span alternate lines.

'I like these 'cos they rhyme,' he announced finally. Then he began to recite his own verse, declaiming it in a sing-song Southern accent, looking ahead, but watching carefully out of the corner of his eye to see how I was reacting.

I mean – what do you do when you're sitting crouched under a mammoth who put Sonny Liston away in Round Two? It's not exactly the place to tell him his poems don't work. But in fact here and there were lines which could stand on their own – even if they weren't written by a heavyweight champ.

> 'The same road that connects
>   two souls together.
> When stretched becomes a
>   path to God.'

or

'When the ears of the heart
Can sense the ears of other
     hearts
Words become unnecessary.'

Ali kept the poetry recital going for an hour. Sitting in the next seat, I was able to have a close-up view of his face – unlined despite punches that would have left another man's face like Limerick Lace. His ears are close to his head, neat and well-formed. Long fingers, powerful, but with a touch of elegance. When he straightens up in his seat you can see his trousers stretched tightly over gigantic thighs which are more than two feet in circumference.

I asked him how he could remember so much of his own verse.

'When I go up to Pennsylvania to work out and give up eating pork (this is because of his Muslim beliefs) I just fill up with words.'

He told me calmly he would beat Foreman – no bombast now. (We were, after all, fellow poets.) He felt Foreman could not hit him.

'I roll with every punch. Something inside tells me it's coming. Then I use my left hand – my best punch. I cut them up with it and then I get to work with both hands.'

He would retire eventually and be a black preacher for his people. 'They need so much,' he said, almost wistfully. A troubled look came into his eyes.

'They try to pretend "Swing Low Sweet Chariot" is a hymn, but what it really meant for the black people was that they had visions of an army up there in the sky which will destroy the whites.'

His voice grew angry.

'Why do whites think they are superior beings? They have no right. There's thousands of UFO's waiting to come down on cities and blast the whites away.'

I looked at him and wondered was he putting on. There was that boyish glint of fun in his eyes which dilutes his most ferocious statements.

How had he felt when the Boxing Board took his title

away from him because he refused to be drafted into the US
Army?

'I'll tell you something. I just went and did my own thing.
My agent, Dick Fulton, sent me on lecture tours all over the
United States. I got in a Volkswagen and travelled thousands
of miles on my own.'

Wasn't it dangerous by himself in the deep South?

'I could be shot to-morrow if it's the will of Allah. A true
Muslim doesn't fear, neither does he grieve. I was happier
than I've ever been in that little car all by my black self –
laughing, singing and tap dancing wherever I went. Fulton
sent me down there in the middle of all those riots, but
nothing happened. I was one black the State didn't get, who
didn't sell out. I was no Uncle Tom.'

Just before the plane landed I got an insight into the
champ's sense of public relations. As he recited his verse,
some little boys in the seats in front were gazing back
goggle-eyed.

Ali held up his hand majestically. The bard's flow was not
to be interfered with. Finally, one little Jewish boy, greatly
daring, shoved the microphone of a tape recorder under Ali's
mouth. For a second I thought the Champ would explode.
He jumped up.

'I'm going to hit you so hard you'll never get up. I'm
gonna knock you right out of the plane, you great idiot. I'm
gonna do to you what I did to Joe Frazier.'

It was only when I saw a delighted grin on the kid's face
that I realised what Ali had done. He was giving the kid the
thrill of his life by telling him on tape that a heavyweight
champion of the world would knock him out.

As we walked from the plane at Kennedy Airport, everyone recognised Ali. Some reached out to touch him.

'It's hard to be humble when you're as good as I am,' Ali
said as he walked past the fence. 'I'm good-looking. I can
sing, dance, talk. I can box better than anyone else.'

He looked at me sideways, the same boyish glint of
mischief – putting on.

There was a chauffeur-driven Rolls-Royce to meet him
outside. Ali offered me a ride to town. He introduced me to
his broken-nosed companion, who turned out to be Kid

Gavilan, former welterweight champion of the world and master of the 'Bolo' punch. The Kid was down and out in Alabama recently when Ali discovered him and picked up the tab.

As we rolled into Fun City, the Kid started singing Spanish songs which he maintained he had written himself, while Ali's well-shaped head rolled from side to side in the front seat.

The champ was out for the count.

23rd March, 1975

Gorgeous Georges – the last fling

In Paris Peggy Roch of *Elle* magazine said she had seen Georges Carpentier the day before walking in the Tuileries Gardens with his dachshund, Norbert, and looking 'very fit'. That afternoon I went to call on him, as I normally did when I was in Paris. He was out. Two days later I read he was dead.

Carpentier was eighty-one. The last time I saw him, a year ago, he explained his theory of the knock-out. It was worth listening to, because Carpentier's fighting weight was only about 12 stone, but he knocked out most of the leading heavyweights of his day:

'You must aim like a marksman for the point of the chin. If you land, it is the end.'

But what about Bombardier Billy Wells, whom Carpentier put away in less than a minute with a body-punch?

'Well, you see, his weak spot was his stomach, so I lowered my sights.'

Had he ever missed?

'Yes, against Dempsey. I aimed for his chin. Just then he lowered his head. I landed on his cheekbone. I thought I had taken his head off. Then I thought my own hand had come off. Look!'

He showed me his right hand with a lump of scar-tissue over the thumb-joint.

'To-day there is only one puncher – Foreman. Ali is not a puncher.'

To which I could only reply that there weren't many boxers who would exactly relish an Ali haymaker.

'Yes; but what I mean by a puncher is a boxer who can

knock out a man with one punch. Dempsey, Joe Louis, Benny Leonard, Ray Robinson, myself. Regardez!'

He started to glide across the carpet. His right hand was held just below his breast-bone:

'One day I learned that a punch comes from the leg. Then I just send my fist up with a thrust from my right thigh. After that they went out with one blow.'

Carpentier was the best looking boxer in fight history. He had fair golden hair, blue eyes and Greek features. When I last saw him, though he was eighty, his features were unmarked. I reminded him of the gory description Gene Tunney had given of how he had lacerated Carpentier at the Polo Grounds, New York in July 1924. How had he preserved his face with the punishment he was supposed to have taken?

'I will let you into a secret.'

The voice became confidential, very Charles Boyer,

'I always took a dive when I felt I could not win. It is easy to make your nose bleed, you know. Then I would smear it all over my face in between rounds. After that I went down – alors brave Georges.'

Carpentier's glamour was such that women fainted at the ringside at the mere sight of him. After the first few seconds in the ring, his skin became pink in colour. More girls would reach for smelling salts.

'Yes, I was fond of les jeunes filles. I liked to have a new girl once a week when I was training for a fight. Descamps arranged it.'

This at a time when trainers in Britain genuinely believed your toes would fall off if you chased the chicks while in training.

'I also smoked a cigarette before a big fight. It calmed my nerves.'

Carpentier knocked other myths on the head. The Victorian one that Froggies were small, dark, over-sexed and liable to run when confronted by energetic Teutons, for instance. Carpentier went to fight in London looking more Anglo-Saxon than anything Cecil Rhodes could have dreamed up, and put Billy Wells, the pride of Empire, on the canvas in one round. He was to become so popular in England that after he beat Gunboat Smith he had to fight his way through dense crowds from Charing Cross down the Strand to get to his hotel at Northumberland Avenue.

During the First World War he became a pilot in the French Air Force, and won the Croix de Guerre. When it was over, he resumed his boxing and quickly went into the million-dollar class. But though he was light-heavyweight champion of the world, Carpentier never won the heavyweight championship. Why was everyone so crazy about him? Even when he was beaten by Dempsey, Lloyd George telegrammed:

'I admire you more than ever.'

Francois Mauriac, the Nobel Prize-winning novelist, called Carpentier:

'The nearest approach there is to the type of perfect gentleman beloved of Pascal and of the Chevalier de Mère.'

Perhaps, subconsciously, he represented for Europeans the last fling of the old world against the crude success of the new. D'Artagnan against the mongrel horde. But I think above all it was his glamour. I never met anyone who had more of it.

Carpentier lived, like many of his time, with the knowledge of the monstrous dead in the back of his mind. Paris of the Twenties, with its excitement, was one means of forgetting the slaughter that had gone before. 'To astonish' was the maxim of the era. Duchamps would paint a moustache on the Mona Lisa. Dali address the French Academy on the art of the cauliflower, Cocteau announce his wish to catch Nijinsky as he fell from the air in his famous leap, while somewhere along the Left Bank two young writers, Ernest Hemingway and Scott Fitzgerald, were spending their afternoons boxing in the ring.

The age demanded glamour from its personalities; it got it in Chevalier, Colette, Coco Chanel . . . and Georges Carpentier, in some ways the most dazzling of all, the best looker and the hardest hitter pound for pound in the history of the ring.

23rd November, 1975

Rocky Graziano

When I read that 'Rocky' was an Academy Award film, I assumed it was about Rocky Graziano. He was the first Rocky I'd heard of, the one Paul Newman made the movie about, and who'd made more money in middleweight championships bouts than any fighter in history. When I went to see the movie, and discovered it was a fairy tale about a kid from Philadelphia who mumbled worse than Brando and boxed as badly, I was as sore as a lot of real Rocky fans were.

I met Rocky Graziano last week in New York, and asked him what he thought about it. He is a generous guy with brown eyes that do a lot of twinkling. The funny thing is he doesn't give a damn that they stole his name.

In the Friar Tuck restaurant on Third Avenue where he hangs out, Rocky said 'I patented the name in 1942, and I could have sued. But Stallone is a nice kid, and he's making a lot of money. Good luck to him.'

When I'd walked to the restaurant through the streets with Rocky, it was like being with royalty. People bowed to him as he passed. Others came up and put their arms around his shoulders. 'How's it going, Rocky? You look great.'

Rocky nods pleasantly to everyone. He is one of the last survivors of the New York characters who were personalities in the streets of Manhattan – Jimmy Walker, George M Cohan, Jack Dempsey. After his fighting career was over, Rocky made a name for himself as a talk-show star. I could see why as I listened to his conversation at lunch. When I asked him about the fight in which he took the world middleweight championship from Tony Zale, he said:

'That wuzn't a fight, that was war, and if there wasn't a referee, one of the two of us would have ended up dead.'

Rocky's three fights with Zale are remembered as the greatest in the history of middleweight boxing. In the first one in New York in 1946, Zale had Rocky down eight times; but he got up again and again until finally he was chinned in the sixth round. Then, in Chicago a year later, Graziano had his left eyelid torn off, and temporarily lost the sight of his other eye. But in the sixth round he put Zale away. A year later, at Newark, he lost the title after he had crawled up the ropes three times in an attempt to defy Zale's fearful hooks and jabs.

It was a tearaway street fighter against a classic boxer in the Marquess of Queensberry style. Zale's straight lefts were perfectly delivered with a murderous whiplash effect. Rocky, on the other hand, had essentially only one punch, a right hand that appeared to travel in an arc, and which if it connected sent his opponent to Dreamsville (52 out of his 83 fights he won by a KO).

I had watched that punch so often on the movies that I asked Rocky to demonstrate it for me at lunch. With a pleased grin like a cat contemplating a bowl of milk, Rocky lifted his right hand and held it in the same position that a cop would controlling traffic, at his shoulder, fist closed and pointed to the ceiling. Then as it came across the table, I noticed the wind of it disturbed the top of my coffee. Though I knew it wasn't meant for me, I didn't like to think what might have happened if Rocky's aim had been a little off. I could see that it was an orthodox straight right. But it started off away from his right shoulder, which made it look like a loop; then halfway it became the real thing, a killer cross.

Today Rocky Graziano is a rich man:

'I get two thousand dollars a throw when I appear at a banquet. And Mike Douglas has me on his TV show twelve times a year, and I have a contract worked out for that. Also, I do a lot of commercials.'

The reason Rocky is so much in demand is that as soon as his boxing career was over, he made a name for himself as a TV actor:

'Yeah, I did two years on the Martha Raye programme

with people like Cesar Romero and Robert Taylor.'

He is a trim guy today, and plays golf to a 12 handicap three times a week. For someone who got beat up as much as Rocky did, his face is in great shape. He has most of his teeth, good eyes and a fine clear skin that is remarkable in a man of nearly sixty. You notice his manners. He misses nothing. If there was someone who wasn't getting enough attention, Rocky immediately and courteously brought him into the circle.

King Rocky. Like many guys who have got there, he is magnanimous. No nasty tales about rivals:

'Joe Louis is doing great. He was in town yesterday with a limousine to drive him around. I remember a few years ago Joe was acting strange. He used to put sellotape around his room at night to prevent the Feds from listening in. Now he's married to a nice doll on the West Coast who is a lawyer, and she is looking after him.'

Talking to this courteous, amusing gentleman, it is hard to imagine that he spent six years of his life in jail, that society looked on him as a hoodlum. Even after he came out of jail and made it with his fists, Rocky was always getting busted for something or other. In the army he hit a captain, and had to go AWOL. It was then he took the name Rocky Graziano, so that he could fight in the ring and avoid arrest. (He was born Rocco Barbella.)

After Rocky had become middleweight champion in 1946, a reporter asked him in his dressing room what it felt like to be champion.

'I never had nothing. I was always poor. I don't know,' Rocky said. But the reporter persisted. 'I just don't know,' Rocky pleaded. 'I never had nothing.'

Today it's different. He does *have* something – a name that belongs to the history of the game.

8th May, 1977

Randy: the real life Rocky?

Randy Neumann is a handsome six-foot white American with prospects in Hollywood. He is also doing well as a writer. What is unusual about Randy is that he is a boxer who has been ranked sixth in the States and who has a victory over Jimmy Young, the heavyweight who scared the pants off Ali last May by nearly beating him in Washington.

Randy is 'the Baby Hemingway' of the Lion's Head. This is the writer's bar of New York where Norman Mailer, Barbra Streisand, Pete Hamill, Dwight McDonald, Wilfred Sheed, Shirley MacLaine and David Amram hang out. When I got there last week the news was that Randy was going into the ring again after 12 months lay-off in an elimination bout for the world TV championship series.

There was a party for him at the Lion's Head two days before the fight, Randy was looking chipper.

'I have just given my first novel outline to my publishers and they like it,' he told me.

Jimmy Young is due to fight Foremen next month in an elimination bout for the heavyweight title and if he wins the fight Randy would be in the reckoning again.

I asked him how it felt to be a contender. Randy flashed one of those smiles which have made him the darling of women editors of the New York magazines. (*Viva* magazine once printed 14 photographs of Randy in the shower.)

'I get $10,000 for this fight and if I win the series $50,000. That's going to help me do a lot of writing and acting.'

Then another of those smiles which drew a deep sigh from a blonde girl standing right behind me.

'Oh, Randy, those photographs in *Viva*! Why did you get yourself photographed in the next issue with a girl? I tore you up after that.'

Randy was smiling like a strobe light and the girl was clinging on to him when I moved off to get my ticket for the fight. The entire writing fraternity from the Lion's Head were going out next day in a bus to New Jersey to cheer for Randy.

Everyone was excited as the bus headed off. It would be nice to have a writer-champ about the bar again. There was a lot of beer in the bus and people seemed to be smoking something that smelled sweet.

The atmosphere at the fight was like something out of a 1930s movie. Guys were standing up in their seats shouting and there were large men chewing cigars. In the back seat was an enormous blind man with a seraphic smile on his face who cocked his ear to the roar of the crowd as he listened with the other one to an account of the fight from a pal next to him.

An MC with a face of a well made up corpse, announced the fight in funereal tones. There were boxing groupies in the front row who kissed and shrieked whenever their favourite boxer went on a rampage.

When Randy's fight against Sailor Arrington was announced a surprise was that Angelo Dundee, Muhammad Ali's trainer, was in the Sailor's corner. The Sailor was a tough-looking customer with a chin which seemed to be permanently fixed to his chest.

In the first round Randy came out with classic straight lefts knocking the Sailor's head back like an Aunt Sally. It was like Muhammad Ali against Jean Pierre Coopman, the flat-footed Lion of Flanders.

Randy danced around on his toes as his opponent flailed at him. I don't know if boxers think of such things during fights but if Randy won this one he could be in line for $50,000.

Then in the second round disaster struck. Suddenly Randy's left eye seemed to have been designed by Francis Bacon. He had taken a butt from his opponent which cut him right across the eyelid. At the end of the round, the seconds monkeyed around with him, but it was clear from now on that he couldn't see from one eye. He wasn't able to judge his distance. In fact I learned afterwards that it was worse, he had double vision. In the fifth round with a half blind man in the ring, the referee stopped the fight.

I went into the dressing room to see Randy. He didn't look downhearted at all, though his right eye was a red blotch.

'I have really got a sense of relief. There's no way you can avoid this in a fight. Everytime I go into a ring I can meet a bozo like Arrington who will cut me. Now I can plug back into my acting and writing activities.'

On the way back on the bus they weren't talking too much. Someone said that Randy had always been a cutter. Against Chuck Wepner, who fought Ali for the world title, Randy was ahead five rounds when the fight stopped because of a cut eye.

Back in the bar there wasn't much talk about the fight either. A film director was on the phone explaining to the operator he wanted Istanbul not Englewood Cliffs. Someone else was saying Manson was innocent. They would have to save up their talk about this fight until it became a legend. It would be a long time before the Lion's Head bred another 'Baby Hemingway'.

24th April, 1977

Jack Dempsey

Jack Dempsey owns a restaurant on Broadway and I went to see him in his milieu. Whatever they say about brain damage in boxing the guy looked perfect. Although he's nearly eighty he looked closer to seventy years of age.

The only boring thing was that he was in the company of a pussycat of a woman who wanted to answer all the questions. I pointed out that I came to interview the Champ, not her.

'Then a good interview you vill not have' she said in a foreign accent. I looked at Jack. He didn't exactly wink. But the message was clear. Stuff her.

He wasn't anxious to talk about his fights. Whether Carpentier hit him on the cheekbone or the chin. He had said it too often before.

But he was able to recall the famous long count in the Championship fight with Tunney when he failed to go to his corner after knocking down his opponent and threw away the fight.

'I thought he was knocked out. I hit him seven times when he was going down with all the punches I had tried to hit him with in my sleep in the past year.' (Tunney when I asked him about this, denied that he was even dazed. 'Irishmen don't get knocked out' was his bland comment.)

'Who was the best fighter you ever fought?'

'Jack Sharkey.'

'A Lithuanian, despite his Irish name.'

'Well, I was no Lithuanian. My grandparents came from County Kildare. My grandad used to tell me about Ireland. His son, my father, was a schoolteacher.'

'Did your Dad not try to stop you taking up prize fighting?'

'Not at all. He was Irish and the fight game was a good career for an Irishman then. The best fighters were Irish, from Jim Corbett down, whom I met once by the way and who was a very fine gentleman and boxer.'

Jack Dempsey learned to box from his brother Bernard, who was also a prize fighter, but with a glass jaw.

Looking at the mammoth jaw across the table it was hard to imagine that anyone in the family could have been weak in that department.

'What age are you, Jack?'

'Seventy-nine.' There was a hiss like steam escaping from a pipe from the left.

'Eighty-one.' She had put Jack Dempsey in his place. The broad looked pleased but he didn't.

'I was born in 1895,' he said apologetically, as if his authenticity and not his ladyfriend was at fault. He actually looks about seventy.

His hair was wavy black with grey streaks. Clear blue eyes. Not a trace of the pug in his striking full fingers, like a pianist. Small undecipherable knuckles. Except when they reach the wrist. Then they turn into something which looks like a mixture of bog oak and granite.

'Best punch?'

'Left jab. Can't be a Champ without it.'

'You had a reputation as a two-fisted fighter?'

'That's because I was two things. I used to fight a boxer and box a fighter.'

He laughed. His extraordinary charm bathed the restaurant for a moment. It is something you find in big men who have been champions; the adulation they have had breeds such confidence that aggression, the counterpart of charm, drains out of them.

When he stood up to go he loomed over me. A mighty man. There had been no champion in any game like him. Whenever a boxer wins a world heavyweight title, the first thing the journalists still ask is could he have beaten Dempsey in his prime.

Even in Sweden when he got off the plane with Ingemar Johannsson it was Dempsey the crowd went for, not Ingo.

Now as he sat in the restaurant, people bowed to him as they passed as if he was a saint or guru.

He carved his legend when there was no television at a time when he was able to make a million pounds a fight for proving that he could lick anyone in the world with his bare hands.

'O.K. champ,' he said as I left.

I looked at the blonde. She was talking vigorously to a companion. But I could have sworn as I went out that fury was making her ears wag.

December, 1977

The artist who discovered beauty in boxing

Last month at the exhibition of American Art at the Whitney Museum in New York I noticed a crowd round one picture. It was a painting of the Dempsey–Firpo World Heavyweight boxing bout by George Bellows. Bellows had been at the ringside when he made the sketches for the painting, so close that Dempsey actually fell in to Bellows's lap when he was knocked out of the ring in the first round by Firpo, the Wild Bull of the Pampas. Bellows told his friends afterwards that he 'placed Dempsey carefully back in the ring with instructions to be of good cheer'.

He would have been surprised, even then, that his painting of the fight would be chosen to represent him in a retrospective exhibition of American Art between 1920–1945, for he was recognised previously as a major painter in landscape and portraiture. He caught the dancing marine light of New York City in his paintings of the Hudson River, and critics compared him with Hogarth for his savage depictions of life in the slums or his drawings of lunatics in the madhouses.

However, he was particularly well suited by his background to paint pictures with a sporting background. At Ohio State University Bellows had been a star at baseball and basketball. When he came into the arena the crowd would chant 'Hoh Bellows', which was sometimes changed to 'Belly Ho'. A contemporary recalled the artist engaged in another sport, 'the indescribably beautiful gesture as Bellows threw the ball to first baseman's glove'.

Early on Bellows recognised the aesthetic element in sport. 'There is no music so beautiful,' he wrote, 'as the ring of a good bat meeting the ball on its dear little cheek, when you play the tune yourself.'

It was natural then that when he went to New York to be a painter, he would support himself by playing professional baseball. Very soon he established himself as a leading painter with his contemporaries Edward Hopper and John Sloan. At the age of twenty-nine his paintings were hung in the famous 69th Armoury Exhibition, when America was shocked by its first glimpse of Picasso and Matisse, and by Marcel Duchamps's 'Nude Descending Staircase'.

After the First World War his popularity declined, perhaps because he espoused the Socialist cause, which hardly endeared him to the rich, who were his best customers. But his boxing lithographs were hung in clubs and bars throughout the United States. The most famous ones were 'Stag at Sharkeys' and 'Club Night' which were followed by the Dempsey–Firpo painting.

In 1924 Herbert Bayard Swope commissioned Bellows to draw sketches of the Dempsey–Carpentier fight for the New York World newspaper. No painter has ever caught as Bellows did the coiled fury and curved perfection of boxers' bodies as they hurl themselves against one another.

When criticised once for depicting a fight that he hadn't attended, Bellows replied: 'I wasn't aware that Leonardo had a ticket of admission for the Last Supper.'

However, for the Dempsey–Firpo fight, he made hundreds of drawings of the two boxers before he finally finished the painting. He allowed himself a slight departure from realism in the finished work. He painted himself in at the extreme left of the picture, instead of in the centre where Dempsey fell out of the ring. His masterpiece proved the truth of what his teacher, Robert Henri, had told him: 'There is beauty in everything if it looks beautiful to *your* eye.'

7th May, 1978

Muhammad Ali v Jimmy Young

Muhammad Ali looked bored getting into the ring at Land-over, Maryland. He's had too many fights that he knew he couldn't lose. He is only overweight from eating ice cream and cakes. But his wind is excellent, and his legs and arms are in shape. Or they were before Jimmy Young, his 'no hope' challenger, got to work to take the great man the full 15 rounds.

Ali won all right, by a unanimous verdict, but not clearly. Never mind, his entourage remains black and beautiful – some of the most gorgeous ladies in the United States, brown, black and saffron, every kink out of their hair, dressed out of Paris. Drama is generated like an atomic reactor from the champ's room. In the afternoon, Governor Jerry Brown of California, en route to a pugilistic putsch in the primaries, called in just to have his photo taken with Ali.

Ali took so long to get up steam in the fight, that in the end he could have lost. He just couldn't get through Young's guard. He missed completely with some right crosses, and had to resort to rabbit punches with the inside of the glove, a lazy man's tactic. Young can duck well, fade out of distance. His weakness is that he has a poor left lead, and stands square. He had never fought more than ten rounds before this, and Ali obviously felt he'd chin him around that time.

In the ninth round, Ali got up off his heels on to the balls of his feet, always a sign that he's sniffing around for the kill. Dancing to the left, he flicked out ten left jabs in succession. But they didn't get him far. Points – but no damage. By round eleven he was down on his heels again, plodding after Young and concerned about winning.

Then, in round twelve Young was up on his toes and starting to move around as if cheered by his discovery that he could last the distance. He was weaving well, and Ali, throwing in some vicious crosses, missed with all of them.

In the thirteenth round, it was Young who put in the right crosses, and twice he landed smack on Ali's chin and shook him. In the fourteenth Young definitely set the pace with more right crosses that hit the target, and a left–right combination that had Ali confused. In the last round, Young seemed so pleased to have lasted the distance that he took no chances with Ali's terrific onslaught, and just stuck his head through the ropes, where he couldn't be got at, as things hotted up. Previously his maximum earnings for a fight were £3,500, but when he left the ring this time he had earned £42,000.

Afterwards, Ali admitted that Young had dazed him. A significant phrase slipped into Ali's monologue: 'I could see Youth facing me.' That is the spectre haunting every champion who has been there a long time – of a fighter with fire in his belly who wants to win more than the champ himself does.

In a preliminary bout, Ken Norton had ripped Ron Stander to pieces with a fusilade of uppercuts that would have taken the head off a hippopotamus. Ali must know he's on a to a toughie here. (Norton broke Ali's jaw in 1973.)

During the boring parts of the fight I was grateful for Elaine. I discovered her of all places purring at my feet. She was one of the beautifully dressed black girls who had been around at the start but there was a mix-up and she hadn't been given a seat, so she sneaked into the press area and was coiled up like a comfortable cat under my table peering up at the fight. I uncoiled her after my foot bumped against her and offered her the press seat next to me. She announced to surprised pressmen that she would cover the fight for the *Virgin Press*.

Then she showed me some photographs of herself and Ali. She was 5 ft 11 in in the colour of coffee ice-cream and luscious. Some journalists behind us shouted at her to sit down when things got exciting – two of them for some reason were covering the fight for *The Economist* – and she turned and fixed them with a look of sweet contempt:

'If y'awl don't stop shouting, I'm going to have to ask you an embarrassing question about your mothers.'

2nd May, 1976

What causes a knock-out?

There has been a good deal of discussion recently in *The Lancet* on the subject of concussion and the danger of ignoring it on the sports field. At one time I had a particular interest in finding out what caused a 'knock-out' as I was appearing regularly in the ring. My father took the *British Medical Journal*, so I used to grab it as soon as it arrived in the hope of finding out useful information on the matter.

The trouble was that the medical theories as to how the knock-out occurred were as diffuse as those about the existence of space men. From the *British Medical Journal* I learned that Pfiffer (1922) thought that the cause of the knock-out was a short-lived obstruction of the jugular vein; Flint (1930) believed that a distortion of the jaw produced a cerebral anaemia; Somen (1930–7) held (with Babinski concurring) that the KO took place in the outer ear; while La Cava (1957) maintained that a blow on the mandible on the side of the jaw led to a drop in nerve-pressure. Barring the possibility that you were an octopus, it seemed impossible to concoct blows that would land in all these places at the same time.

Also, none of these medical theories seemed to coincide with a piece of empirical knowledge I gained when I was eighteen in a boxing booth in Louvain, Belgium. I got to be there because that afternoon I had made a pig's ear of the pole vault at an International Student Games, and was looking for some way to work off my fury.

There was this ferocious Belgian who was offering a fiver to anyone who could put him down in three rounds, and in a rash moment I offered to take him on. A number of locals were coming out of the booth with lopsided jaws, which naturally encouraged my team-mates to persuade me to get in to the ring. It was about twice the size of a normal ring, so I was able to dodge my massive opponent for the first round. Then, coming off the ropes in the second round, by a sheer fluke I caught him with the hardest punch I would ever land in a fight. I waited for him to fall, hoping I hadn't maimed him for life. All he did was grin and say affectionately: 'Iss no good, sonny. I don't fall.' Which was true. I could have hit him on the chin with a sledge-hammer, and it wouldn't have had any effect.

Afterwards, in his den, he gave me a drink. He had been active in the Belgian Resistance and, assuming I was English, explained to me with enthusiasm how he used to break the necks of German storm-troopers who gave him trouble. I asked him his secret. He took me outside and showed me an enormous cannonball. Attached to it was a rope which he suspended around his neck so that he could lift the cannonball with his neck. I noticed his neck muscles. They were massive. It would have taken two collars of mine placed end to end to go round it. 'Iss the secret,' he explained, patting his neck.

Some time after I had given up boxing, I came across a paper written in 1943 by an Oxford scientist which seemed to coincide with what the Belgian had told me. The scientist, A. H. Holburn, was investigating brain damage in car accidents, and he concluded that what caused it was not the force of the impact, but the speed at which the head was accelerated on the shoulders. In other words, a ferocious blow in which the head was braced to remain steady would have little effect compared with one which made the head move rapidly in one direction. If a boxer, therefore, had a weak neck, or was caught in a position where his neck-muscles were relaxed, he was liable to be knocked out.

Holburn explains his theory by comparing the human brain to a jelly. If you throw a jelly in the air, it will change shape. In the same way, if the head is accelerated rapidly on the shoulders, according to Holburn, the brain will change shape. This causes what he describes as 'shear strain', or a tearing of the nerve ends. What is interesting is that according to Holburn it is not the force of the blow that matters. He found that it would require a compressive force almost beyond human strength to injure brain cells. What really counts is how fast your head is moved by the blow. In other words, if you keep your neck stiff and your head from rocking, the effect of a blow can be reduced to a minimum.

If Holburn's theory is correct, then the chances of concussion should be minimised by neck exercises which would help to keep the head from spinning when it comes in contact with ball or glove. My Belgian boxing-booth friend in the hard school of experience may have stumbled on a principle that a scientist would later propound after years of patient analysis in the laboratory.

7th December, 1975

Ulick O'Connor, aged 18, in St. Mary's College First Fifteen and (*below*) Irish Universities Welter-weight Boxing Champion.

Ulick O'Connor, aged 18, keeping wicket for University College, Dublin, First Eleven and (*below*) in the same year, Irish Pole Vault Champion.

Ulick O'Connor, aged 44, marking Stanley Matthews with Peter Farrell, formerly of Everton, playing for Old Ireland against Old England.

(*Right*) The reason Ulick O'Connor took up soccer. F. P. – French Olympic High Jumper.

John Flanagan,
winner of three
Olympic medals for
hammer throwing.

'Cannonball Kevin' –
Dr Kevin O'Flanagan
– in his youth when
he won international
caps for both rugby
and football.

Abbé Pistre the
outspoken rugby
commentator.

Left: Nobel Prize winner Samuel Beckett, a man of letters and of sport and (*below*) Group Captain Sir Douglas Bader DFC, DSO, the legendary fighter pilot. (*Opposite page*) Henri La Mothe diving in front of Independance House, Philadelphia.

Suzy Chaffee – beauty
on skis.

GOLF

Sir Douglas Bader

'It's pissing rain, old boy, we can't play.'

Instead of having 18 holes with a sporting legend, I was having coffee with him. You are struck by the youthfulness of his face and smooth, flawless skin. No lines, but a serenity you see in monks, or ascetics who live on the sides of mountains in India. His hair is still darkish, which makes him look a handsome fifty, though he will be seventy-one in February.

I've never been able to understand how, with two artificial legs, Douglas Bader could have played to a four-handicap and drive a golf ball on average 240 yards.

'Timing, old boy. But it took me hundreds of attempts before I even hit my first ball. I fell on my behind every time. But I knew how to fall from gymnastics, which was invaluable. After that, I would play one hole and then go back to the clubhouse. By a stroke of luck, you could arrive at the clubhouse from almost every hole at Fleet, so there were great celebrations when I finally made 18 holes.'

I looked at his wrists. They were like a blacksmith's. Powerful hands, freckled. How did he keep those splendid shoulders so firm these days?

'Well, you see, I swing myself along on my hands when I go for a bath. Then I hoist myself into the bath. I don't put on these things until later.'

He put his hand on one of 'these things'.

'The right one is a quarter-of-an-inch shorter than the left. I was playing a round one day with Henry Longhurst when I found I could hit the ball better if I had an uphill lie. So I

thought, why not have a permanent uphill lie by getting my
right leg shortened? I rang Henry after I'd done this, and he
shouted into the 'phone: "But you've altered the wrong leg".
He never got it right to his dying day.'

Bader laughed; an incongruous haw-haw which contrasts
with the elfin glint in his eyes. He radiates fun, and peppers
his conversation with witty references. An accountant is
described as: 'One of those fellows with thin lips you
couldn't squeeze a lima bean through.'

In December, 1931, when he woke and found he'd lost his
legs, Douglas Bader knew his chances of playing rugby for
England were over. The month before that, he'd played for
the Combined Services against the touring Springboks.

'I would have played for England. I don't mind saying it
now. The chap I displaced in the Combined Services was the
England fly-half the year before.'

Rugby correspondents at the time wrote a lot about
Bader's 'marvellous hands', and against Cambridge in October of 1931, playing for the Harlequins, he scored three tries.

'I couldn't watch rugby for years after I lost my legs. Not
till my contemporaries had finished playing anyway.'

To-day he is a keen fan. Barry John particularly fascinated
him.

'He only moved his legs when he ran. The top part of his
body was still. That made it easier for him to deceive an
opponent. But the best three-quarter line I ever saw was the
Oxford one: Smith, Macpherson, Aitken and Wallace. Wallace used to lengthen his stride and keep the same leg beat,
and so just used to float out of the full-back's hands without
even having to swerve.'

Bader was one of the great all-rounders. At Cranwell, he
got Blues for cricket, rugby, hockey and boxing. He was
never beaten as a middle-weight boxer, and won all his
nineteen fights with knock-outs.

'I think I still hold the record at Sandhurst for a knock-out.
I got a fellow in seven seconds after the bell went. A
wonderful sergeant told me before I went in, "Hit him in the
guts, sir, and then climb up to the attic".'

He once took five wickets and made 171 in an inter-
squadron cricket match. Once playing cricket at school, he

bowled out a boy in a class above him named Laurence Olivier.

'Larry told me years later he was dreaming as he went out to the wicket, as little boys do, of playing for England: then I put him out first ball. Do you know, he was so good at acting in school plays, he seemed to be over-acting, he was so much better than anyone else.'

We talked about poetry. Bader had read a lot of it in bed while he waited to get mobile on his artificial legs.

'I like Swinburne very much, Keats, Robert Service, and an Australian called Banjo Patterson, in fact any poet with a rhythm that flows off your tongue.'

Unlike Swinburne, who was a teenage wino, Bader has never drunk alcohol.

'Don't like the taste. Tried them all, gin, whisky, wine. Simply didn't like them.'

It's typical of his individual outlook. He was once described as being 'driven by a demon of egoism, harnessed to causes and achievement'. But it is a demon that leaves lots of time for fun, and works itself out at helping a number of people with the same problems as he has.

'I would do anything for charity barring baring my behind on a stage.'

Being with him is so much of a lark that you can forget the steel in his character that made him the third man in history to get a bar to the DFC and DSO, and drove him to walk again on the stumps of his shattered legs so that he not only played championship golf, but squash and tennis as well. He has flown so often near the sun that he has made the clouds on the brink seem insignificant.

'You know,' said the hotel porter, as Bader strode off to the swing doors of the Park Lane, 'I saw him thirty years ago come out of the Berkeley into a taxi in three giant strides like an antelope. I thought he was going to come out the other side. There's nothing like him, sir, or ever will be.'

2nd November, 1980

Harry Bradshaw – putter of genius

Bernard Darwin called Portmarnock golf course 'one of the few unquestionably great golf links in the world'.

Laid out in 1894, it is on a peninsula 10 miles from Dublin city centre. The sea is at your side as you drive off from most of the tees. The clubhouse rises like a Venetian palace from the waves as you approach from Baldoyle; a little gem with a miniature clock tower. John Betjeman, who played here when he was in the Legation in Dublin during the war, might have noticed it more.

One of the charms of the place is that you can meet Harry Bradshaw, who is the professional there. Harry is remarkably like Mr Pickwick these days; smiling, cherubic, rotund. He won the Canada Cup with Christy O'Connor in 1958, (the only pair from these islands to do this) and tied for the Open with Bobby Locke in 1949 before losing the play-off.

Two months ago Harry equalled the world record for putting. He went round Portmarnock in nineteen putts. He had fifteen one-putts, two two-putts and holed out on one green with a chip.

I played a round with him on Tuesday to see how it was done. When he putts he appears to barely touch the ball. His back-swing is almost imperceptible. Then he brushes it in with his right hand, 'plenty of follow-through'.

He believes in putting with wrists only. On the eighteenth as he sank a 30-footer he explained that whenever he gets on a green he aims to hole in one whether he's twenty yards or two yards away from the hole.

This stern ambition came as a result of his friendship with a

Delgany priest, a Father Sean Scannell. One day after a rash of three putts Father Scannell said, 'That won't do, Harry.'

He decided that from now on Harry must hole out in one no matter where he landed on the green. Even if the ball was 50 feet from the hole, the patient priest would wait until Bradshaw got the ball in. It often took a long time. Father Scannell sat on a camp chair reading his breviary till the ball went down. One game took 6½ hours.

'After that,' Bradshaw recalls, 'he made me promise to practise an hour a day, and I did though it nearly broke my back.'

The result affected his whole game.

'I never had to worry about my second shot as long as I was anywhere near the green. I could always get down with a chip and a putt.'

For a player of world class there has always been something agricultural about Bradshaw's golf swing. This was acquired in his passion for accuracy. He found it one day in the 'bunch of grapes grip' which results in a swing rather like a street sweeper brushing leaves into his cart. His right hand almost completely covers his left one.

'The day I found that grip, I could hit through the eye of a needle. I kissed my hands and said you're my baby for the rest of my life.'

His relaxed outlook stood by him when he was involved in the most bizarre incident in the history of championship golf. In 1949 while playing in the Open at Royal St George's on the fifth hole in the second round he drove into the rough and found his ball in a broken bottle. Most golfers would have been apoplectic. Bradshaw laughed. The Irish side of him was struck by the ridiculousness of the situation. But when he had finished laughing there was a problem.

Was he allowed to pick up without losing a stroke? In fact he would have been but there were no officials present, only a fifteen-year-old whom Daddy had asked to mark the card. After waiting 20 minutes Bradshaw, turning his head away from the ball to avoid the flying glass, hit it 15 yards. His first round had been 68. The bottle incident made the second one 77. Yet he finished with rounds of 68 and 70 to tie with Bobby Locke.

In the play-off Locke won. As they walked in Locke remarked to a pressman that Bradshaw was smiling so much that it was hard to tell who lost. He beat Locke in the Irish Open a month later at Belvoir Park, Belfast. Then he won the Dunlop Masters in 1953 and 1955.

As you play with him he tells you funny stories and chats away. He had a hole-in-one when he was nine and won a Woodbine which made him sick, so that he never smoked again. When he and Christy O'Connor arrived late on a plane for the Canada Cup, a Mexican official said, 'the last shall be first' and bought them champagne when the result proved him right. If Bobby Locke was putting, he says, and you threw pebbles, 'the ball would jump over them'.

He is so easy-going it is hard to see him in the ruthless mould of championship golf. But there is a tough streak there. It comes out in his attitude to drink. Though he is not a teetotaller Harry will refuse to drink with the lads if he doesn't want a jar. Though it has made him unpopular sometimes, Harry Bradshaw doesn't give a damn. He works things his own way which is how he learned to putt and swing.

As I was leaving he was rooting in the back of his car for something. I thought he was going home. He came up with an old putter and Harry Bradshaw, who is sixty-three this year, said he was going out to do an hour's practice on the putting green.

21st November, 1976

Record holder in the long drive

Tommie Campbell has driven a golf ball further than any-body alive and doesn't know how it's done. He is 10 stone 6 and 5 feet 8½ inches in height, with small hands like a boxer's, not the big hams golfers often have.

'Are those fellows who throw the javelin big?' he said in a puzzled voice as we walked out on the fourteenth tee at Castle Golf Club, Rathfarnham last week – we were playing the long holes only, to give room for Tommie's drives.

I said javelin throwers come in all sizes.

'Then I don't know what it is,' he said with a resigned shrug. 'When I was nine I went in for a cricket ball throwing competition at Tullamaine Preparatory School and threw the ball out of the grounds and it was never found again. Then I tried boxing and at 5 stone 7 I knocked a fellow out with my first punch, and his mother started screaming "get that animal out of here".'

He teed the ball high and he hit it 315 yards down the fairway. What was curious was it didn't look a different swing from any other, except that there was more of a swish sound at the end. He was down in 3 with a chip and a putt on a 4 par hole.

I thought I'd watch more carefully on the next drive as we moved to the 504 yards sixteenth. This time I noticed he didn't let the clubhead touch the ground before addressing the ball. He goes back as far as possible on the wind-up. He is extremely supple at the waist so he can get his left shoulder round and up without any strain. Then the club comes down with the same swishing sound and the ball flew up and landed

325 yards away. He looked more than ever like a little boy who has just found a toy that works better than anyone else's and doesn't know how it's done.

'How is it that those big fellows who could go through a wall in five seconds often can't hit a ball 150 yards?' he said.

A car tooted him from the nearby roadway.

'That's the Rasher Ryan,' he said with a grin, 'a great character.'

Does he get a lot of people coming up to him because of his famous drive?

'Yes, in Dublin everybody knows you. A fellow even offered me £5,000 for the ball I made the record with, but believe it or not, Dunlop lost it.'

He took a 5 iron out and smacked his second shot on to the green. It was a five par 504-yard hole.

Did he have to take much stick from golfers?

'You often hear fellows saying "oh, that's Campbell at it again", but I have to live with it.'

For a second the grin disappeared from his face.

'Sometimes I'd like to plant them one.'

After he putted for a four I asked him about his golf background.

'Didn't hold a golf club till I was over twenty-five. Father wanted me to go straight into business after I left High School, but I was a sports fanatic and wanted to be a professional cricketer. I played cricket for Merrion at eighteen and got an inter-pro but I chucked the game when I took up golf. I went from 18 handicap to 4 in a year and then to 1, where I've remained since.'

Today at fifty-one, he's owner and managing director of T.C. Carpets Limited, a highly successful floor covering and carpet firm, but he manages to make time to play golf at the top. In 1973 he opened the La Manga course in Spain with Gary Player in a pro-am and had a 66 to Player's 69. Player, who was constantly outdriven by Campbell during the round, said afterwards:

'That's the best amateur I've ever played with.'

We teed up at the seventeenth. Tommie explained that at one time he was able to keep his left heel on the ground at the top of the swing. This gave him the effect of being coiled up like a spring.

He does seem to wind up as he addresses the ball, his legs going into a slight crouch as he begins the back swing. But the remarkable thing is that despite the power that is generated in the clubhead there isn't the slightest indication of force, only a smooth rhythmic movement, like the pendulum of a grandfather clock.

'So straight you could hang your washing on it,' he said with satisfaction as we walked up to this one. 320 yards away.

I asked him if he had felt any different when he drove 392 yards on the eighteenth green at Dun Laoghaire golf course in July 1964.

'I didn't even know it had gone further than usual. Then someone said "cripes, that's a big one". They measured it with chains and it turned out to be a whopper.'

He gave a delighted little-boy grin at the recollection, still unsure how it happened.

Had he entered any driving competitions since?

'Yes, I did win one in Dalton, Georgia, against Bobby Nichols, Bert Yancey, Johnny Pott and others in 1970. I drove 315 yards but it was against the wind. That makes a hell of a difference with these little things.'

He put one of these little things on the second tee. (We were still skipping holes to avoid winging unwary golfers who might be in front of us), and drove off. This one seemed to have a double flight, going low at first and then taking off as if it had a secondary rocket to project it. There wasn't a breath of wind and it landed 350 yards away.

'Norris McWhirter told me I must have been born with an arm like Jimmy Wilde, the KO expert, who was only seven stone. It must be something like that,' he said as we walked to the clubhouse after he had putted for a 4.

I thought of the taxi driver the night before who said when I told him I was going to play with Tommie Campbell:

'For Jesus sake, that drive of his bounced off a stone.'

That's Dublin for you. The only city in the world that has produced three Nobel prizewinners for literature and where every yobbo thinks that he can do better, and where they tell you now that their only record holder in golf bounced the ball off a stone to make his record-breaking drive.

9th August, 1981

Wonky and his rival

When I heard someone say the other day that if the oil crisis got worse golf balls could become like gold, I remembered the war years and the awful feeling you got when your ball sailed towards the rough. If it was lost the game was over for the day.

I was a schoolboy then and there was no hope of getting the father to dig into his precious stock until the following day. New golf balls were unobtainable in neutral Ireland, isolated on the edge of war-torn Europe.

To make it worse, on the seaside course where I played on holidays the rough often grew to the size of small forests; and there was no petrol to work the mowing machines. I have never forgotten the sight of Cecil Ewing, the Walker Cup captain, his bald head almost submerged in ferns before playing what seemed an impossible shot. There was a sound like a helicopter rotor and presently a barrow-load of ferns was dispatched towards the pin with the ball inside, out of which it trickled to the edge of the hole.

On a course with such hazards the lost ball rate was enormous. This is where Wonky came in. He was a dog of indifferent breeding, but with a nose like a geiger counter when it came to locating golf balls. If it wasn't for Wonky golf might have stopped altogether on the course. His master would dispatch him into the giant ferns. A short while later there would be a sharp, pleased yelp. When you went in Wonky would be standing over a ball, while his tail swished happily against the ferns.

Since Wonky was his master's sole means of subsistence

there was understandable jealousy when a rival arrived at the course. This was not, curiously enough, another dog, but a bank manager who seemed to have developed a similar sense of smell.

He used to pace the course from early morning sniffing like a retriever. Then, in the evening, he would come into the clubhouse whistling contentedly with his satchel full of golf balls. These he would take out and scrub in front of the members, who surveyed him with cold fury.

No one spoke to him, of course. Golfers encountering him on the course would cut him. Yet the peculiar thing is that he seemed to attract golf balls. No matter how hard you tried to drive in the opposite direction there was always a tendency to hit towards him. There was almost no part of the course where he could not be seen from, usually standing on a hillock silhouetted against the sky. He was thin and very tall, and had a hooked nose. Some members thought he held his hands like talons. After you had looked for your ball for some time and had failed to find it in the ghastly rough, you'd move off. Then he'd descend, nostril to the wind. In a few seconds he would have another ball in his satchel.

Desperate measures were taken to quench him. Caddies were given a driver on the tee and told to drive straight at him. Members spotting his bony features poking through the ferns would immediately send in low raking shots hoping to wing him. But no one ever scored a bull. His sense of survival was as acute as his sense of smell.

Then a rather awful thing happened. Perhaps through a sense of inferiority from being confronted with a human rival, Wonky lost his sense of smell. The unfortunate dog would just look up plaintively at his master, panting heavily when he was ordered to go in and fetch a ball.

The members became desperate. Without the supply of balls brought in by Wonky there would be little golf that summer. A Dublin surgeon, noted for savage decision in the operating theatre, came up with a plan. He had lost nine balls in two days: and one night he had to be restrained from attacking the bank manager with a mashie in the locker room.

The surgeon went on to the tee with a ball which had been

chewed for a while by his bulldog, an animal who had to have a poker inserted between his jaws to open them on an occasion when he had been reluctant to release a caddy's calf muscle.

The ball had so many tartels flying out of it that only a man of super-human strength could have driven it over a hundred yards. But the surgeon was like a whirling dervish as he swung at it. In his frenzy he managed to land it near enough to the familiar figure on the hillock. A pretence of looking for the ball was made and the party moved off.

Our man swooped. He raised his nostril to the wind and then made for what he thought was a new ball. He fished around for a while. Then a howl of rage was heard. He knew he'd been had. Members popped up from all around where they had been hiding themselves. They gloried in his humiliation and jeered him with the malice of the dispossessed. He looked around at them with a maniacal gleam in his eye. I thought for a moment that he might take off and fly over them in demoniac transformation.

Then he did a rather brave thing. He put the ball in his satchel and walked off with a whistle. Next morning he left on the early train.

Soon Wonky was back in his kingdom sniffing contentedly round the course, reclaiming wealth from the carnivorous rough.

13th July, 1975

GENERAL

Bill Tilden

In 1962 I went to interview Henri de Montherlant, the French dramatist, for the Arts Page of *The Times*. I was wearing a tee-shirt and had cropped fair hair at the time. He took me to be an East German plastic bomber and had me arrested and thrown in jail by the Paris police. Next day the French papers made a great stir. The left-wing ones especially got it up for de Montherlant because he had been friendly to the Germans during the War. They also made a point of his homosexuality which surprised me; de Montherlant had been an Olympic athlete and I didn't think then, that the two went together.

Now another athlete has been brought out of the closet, Bill Tilden, the most famous tennis player in the history of the game. Frank DeFord in his new biography depicts Tilden as a compulsive homosexual with a fondness for teenage lads. Then recently Dave Kopay, former captain of the University of Washington's Rosebowl Football Team and big league professional player, announced that not only was he gay but alleged that a number of other players in the National Football League were as well.

Emile Griffiths, former World Middle and Welter Weight Champion, has never concealed his sexual preferences. He wears diamond studded rings and designs ladies' hats. But when Benny Pareth sneered at Griffiths during the World Title fight for being queer, Griffiths hit him so hard that Pareth died.

One of the ingredients of Thomas Arnold's public school code was the belief that cold showers and vigorous games would separate the guys from the gays. But current scientific studies indicate that Arnold may have been off beam. The guy in the front row with a neck like a rhinoceros could have been the one to be nervous of behind the Fives court, while the languid aesthete out catching butterflies who was allowed off games because of his asthma, was the one who might be chasing your sister on sports day. It was Oscar Wilde walking down Piccadilly with a lily in his hand and in knee breeches who created the image of homosexuality as effeminate. People forgot that Wilde had thrown a number of rowing toughs who came to break up his blue china at Magdalen College, Oxford, down the stairs, while his friend, Lord Alfred ('Bosie') Douglas won a half blue for running at Cambridge.

Frank DeFord in his book on Tilden attempts to explain Tilden's deviation. There are the usual clichés about mother fixation and fear of disease (though why disease should not be passed on by men as well as women is never explained). DeFord really goes over the top, however, when he tells us without a blink that a base ball pitched too hard could set up a castration complex, and that a batsman's failure to hit a ball can lead to impotence. If this idea became current it could cost Kerry Packer a lot of insurance.

Most modern psychiatrists would regard Tilden's case as a matter of hormones. He had an imbalance in this direction and this led to his predilection. It seems clear that in his early years as a tennis champion Tilden was able to sublimate his instincts by acting as a father figure to a host of young tennis players. There is no evidence that he ever propositioned any of them, including Junior Coen whom, at fifteen years of age, Tilden chose to play against China and who is still the youngest Davis Cup player in history. Other Tilden boy protegés were Jack Kramer, and Pancho Segura. In later life, however, Tilden gave free rein to his instincts in a way that had tragic results. In November 1946 he was found in a car on Sunset Boulevard with a fourteen-year-old boy who later involved him in sexual charges. Tilden was jailed for this offence. It doesn't appear to have done much good. Three years later in January 1949 he was arrested again, this time for an offence with a sixteen-year-old hitch-hiker. By now he had become a down-and-out in Hollywood although he still kept up his friendships with film actors like Charlie Chaplin and Joseph Cotten. He continued to play professional tennis and at fifty-eight he was still good enough to beat Frank Parker, the US Amateur Champion, in practice. At the age of sixty he died of a heart attack while preparing to play in the US Professional Championships in Cleveland.

Bill Tilden came from an aristocratic family in Germanstown, Philadelphia, and his father entertained two Presidents, Taft and Roosevelt, at the family mansion, Overleigh. Though Tilden always had a love of tennis, the extraordinary thing is that at the age of twenty-one he was ranked only seventieth in the United States. Four years later he was world champion and became, maybe, the best tennis player of all time. Some tennis experts still claim that no one has ever served a ball harder than he did. It wasn't just his mastery of the strokes, however. He seemed to enter his opponent's mind and anticipate every possible weakness. The game was an art form for him.

'I am doing it for inside of me,' he used to say.

Someone once said about Tilden that he looked on the ball as an individual part of him. Between the ball, himself and an opponent he could choreograph a match like a ballet and give it the brilliance of a Nijinsky.

Tilden had an aristocratic sense of honour, nourished no doubt in the American Prep School, where fair play can take the form of a religion. Imagine a modern player saying to an umpire: 'I won't accept that point,' and then throwing the next stroke if the umpire didn't agree. This is what Tilden did on numerous occasions. He even threw a set in a championship final because he thought his opponent was not getting a fair deal from the Umpire. 'Peach' he would cry if his opponent got in a good shot.

At times he was almost a caricature of an Edwardian sportsman. 'I would rather have you licked like a sportsman than win like a rotter,' he makes a character say in one of his novels.

Altogether Tilden was an *original*. He lived with two maiden aunts, didn't drink and refused to eat vegetables. The only food he ate was steak, ice cream and gallons of black coffee. He wrote plays, some of which were presented on

Broadway, and a few under-rated novels. He appeared on Broadway as an actor and once played Dracula in a film. His books on tennis are classics. To-day, with the evolution of the stage, he could have done a one-man show around his tennis career and acted parts out of his own novels and plays. Temperamentally he was born at the wrong time, even if his tennis fame meant he was received everywhere like a king. The 40s and 50s in America were tough. Tilden's friends, Joseph Cotten and Charlie Chaplin, were being indicted themselves for 'crimes against the State' by the notorious un-American Activities Committee. It wasn't likely that they could afford much sympathy for an aging fag, in trouble with the police for chasing young boys.

One extraordinary fact is that as he grew older, Tilden still retained his youthful appearance. When he started to play in shorts at the age of fifty-five, Gussie Moran sighed, 'God, those legs! Fantastic. Betty Grable should have had them.'

Laid out in an American funeral parlour in a magnificent new sweater bought by Joseph Cotten, he looked little different from Big Bill of the golden days. No representative of the US Tennis Association was at the funeral. Ironically, World Team Tennis to-day bears the same initials as the man who invented the modern game, William Tatem Tilden.

21st August, 1977

Success is a perfect flop

A dive from a 40-foot platform at any time is a feat. Henri La Mothe does it into a pool so small that he can carry it around in a shopping bag. The water he lands in is only 12 inches deep. It barely covers his ankles when he stands up in the pool after the dive.

I should mention that Henri is seventy-one-years old and that he didn't look within ten years of this age when I went to see him at his smart bungalow near Cover, New Jersey, recently. He is able to afford his house in the country because he is paid as much as £300 a dive – not bad for less than two seconds work.

I had phoned him for weeks to catch him. He had been on tour in North Dakota doing his act from city to city. Now he had just come home and was bubbling with energy despite a mammoth drive the night before.

He is a small man with an aristocratic face and darting blue eyes. There is something bird-like about him though his features are too full to make the comparison really apt.

After his Danish wife, Birgit, had made coffee for us, I asked him about his unusual act. Why does he continue these crazy dives at seventy-one years of age?

'I was in vaudeville for years. I liked going around the country. You get addicted to crowds.'

How did he begin?

'Well I was doing something like it for years as a comedy turn in water shows before I discovered that I had an unusual stunt. I used to perform at hotels and country clubs with Johnny Weismuller and Buster Crabbe.

'I would do the comedy turn falling off windows, trees, roofs, into the shallow end of the pool. One day Buster Crabbe said "Cut the comedy and do it straight".'

After that, Henri started to dive into shallower and shallower water. Last year on his seventieth birthday he broke the world record diving from his forty-foot perch into 12½ inches of water outside the Flatiron building in New York, where Harry Houdini once escaped from a strait-jacket hung by his ankles. That dive is now in the *Guinness Book of Records*.

We went next door to a neighbour's house to see video tapes and movies of Henri's dives. As you watch the films, certain things stand out.

Henri crouches on his platform like a crab, waiting for the exact moment to launch himself. When he does take off he goes almost feet first before his body swans out in an exquisite arch like a bird.

'How does the pool look when you are up there?' I asked him.

'A tiny black spot,' he replied. 'It's only 10 feet wide you know. The real trouble is the wind. It could turn me around and around like a leaf.'

Henri claims that he saves himself by landing on his belly, but you feel there is more to it than that. People have been cut in half in less dangerous dives. Yet Henri has never had a scratch.

'It's all in the mind,' he says blandly.

If pressed on the point, he arches his hands and talks about the convex shape of his body muffling the impact. Then, his eyes darting away from you, he will say: 'My only success is a perfect flop.'

You sense he doesn't want to probe too far. It's his secret – and he doesn't even know himself exactly how it's done. It's the sort of feeling you get talking to a Cistercian monk; it's their trip baby – and you're not on it.

Henri La Mothe has had two other careers, on both of which he has left his mark. As a commercial designer he created the 'housing' or cover you see on modern stapling machines. When he was a teenager in his native Chicago he was champion Charleston dancer of the city.

'I used to dance off the stage like an aeroplane, my front hand whirled like a propeller, my head was the motor and my back hand was the tail. This dance became known as the Lindy Hop and swept America.'

At one time Henri had an expensive penthouse studio on West 57th Street, where he worked as a commercial artist and designer.

Then he only did his water stunts on the side. Now he is a full-time professional diver. He drives around the United States in a tiny Renault with his diving pool and ladder on the back seat. He has used his skill as a designer to invent collapsible gear.

'I used to carry my stuff in a trailer; but it was always being broken into. So I designed a pool to fit into a shopping bag and a ladder that folds up as neatly as an umbrella.'

He carries a portable fridge too, so that he can cook his own food in his hotel when he is travelling. He doesn't need to eat much. 'It's all in the mind,' Henri says.

On the way home, I found out how true this was. Though he had just driven back from Sioux Falls in North Dakota, a journey of over 1,500 miles, he had offered to drive me back to New York after we had finished our chat.

It was 2 am. Then Henri, who hadn't made one mistake in his drive across the States, proceeded to get hopelessly lost in Newark's black ghetto. The difference was that, when he had set out to drive from North Dakota, he had concentrated his mind on the job, just as he does when he is gazing at that tiny black spot from his forty-foot perch. Now, chattering away at the wheel, he was no different from the rest of us.

On his perch he is alone with Henri. 'Power goes out of me to intimidate the water,' he says. At that moment, he feels there is nothing he cannot do. He even talks of diving from the Eiffel Tower and the Leaning Tower of Pisa. They burnt men in the Middle Ages for less.

As I said good-bye to him outside the Chelsea Hotel in Manhattan at six o'clock in the morning there were seagulls hopping through the empty streets. Henri looked at them. One of them lifted his head and stared back. It was like to like.

18th May, 1975

Hurling – the fastest field game in the world

At the All Ireland hurling final there were 62,684 people when Cork beat Wexford by 27 points to 23 in what is being regarded as one of the classic games. A foreigner watching the game for the first time could be forgiven for thinking that Harry Houdini had a few relations on the field.

This is the fastest field game in the world and the skill required is fiendish. Once after Martin Coleman, the Cork goalie, had driven the ball (which is the size of a cricket ball) out 90 yards, his team mate, Ray Cummins, swung at it travelling in the air and drove it towards goal where it was slammed, still in the air, by the Wexford fullback and sent back almost to where it came from – nearly 300 yards in less than three seconds – without touching the ground.

A few minutes later Tony Doran ran with the ball balanced on the end of his hurl for 50 yards at full speed.

The clashes at midfield were fearsome. Once Pat Moylan, the Cork midfielder, went for the ball at full speed against Billy Rowsome of Wexford, his hurl held high like a Bengal Lancer. It seemed that there was no way a catastrophe could be avoided. But with a fearful swing in full flight, the wind of which would have flattened a field of daisies, Moylan got the ball clear and himself out of danger.

Ray Cummins, the Cork captain, was the most marked man on the field. When he went for a high ball there were usually four or five with him. There could be a crash like an elm tree falling as the perpendicular hurlys met in mid-air. Yet somehow the ball would come down on one of the hurls; or a hand would shoot up between the sticks and catch the ball rather like a cricketer catching in the deep in the middle of a shower of assegais.

The goal keeping is phenomenal. The goalie has to stop, from point blank range with what amounts to a curved walking stick, a ball coming at him at over 100 mph. It is no wonder that once when a Cork goalie was asked why didn't he stop a ball he replied, 'What is the net for?'

The atmosphere at Croke Park, Dublin, on Sunday was more mid-Atlantic than European. Before the match the teams marched around led by bands and mascots in the American style. The absence of military service in Ireland was evident from the walk of some of the players.

At one time a bishop used to throw in the ball to begin the match and a Faber hymn, 'Faith of our Fathers', exceedingly offensive to Protestants, would be sung. Now theology has been turfed out and the referee throws the ball in without objectionable music. A few years ago they tried opening the game by using a well-known political leader to throw in the ball, but a remark from one of the Greek chorus on Hill 16 put a stop to that, when it was suggested that the politician throw in an anatomical appendage of his own as well and 'make a pawnshop out of the game the same as you made out of the country'.

It is curious that hurling, which continues to draw enormous crowds in the television age in Ireland, has not travelled to other countries. Apart from Scotland it is not played natively anywhere else, although in the eighteenth century a Wexford team used to hurl every year against the Gentlemen of Cornwall and until recently in the Barony of Forth a scythe-shaped hurl was used of the Cornish type.

In Scotland there are 1,000 'camanachd' players, which is Scottish Gaelic for hurling. (In Irish it is 'iománaíocht'.) There have been internationals between the two countries since 1897 and last August a draw of five goals all was the result when they met at Glasgow. The main difference in the Scots game is that there are goals only and no points and they don't catch the ball in the air.

That there is an inherent lure in the game is apparent from the fact that English colonists in Ireland fell for it as far back as the fourteenth century and had to be prevented from playing curling lest it damage Imperial morale; rather as if a Viceroy of India had to be weaned from addiction to snake charming.

One of the Statutes of Kilkenny of 1367 states:

'It is ordained and established that the English do not henceforth use the plays which man call hurlings with grate sticks and a ball on the ground.'

Hurling is the oldest stick game in Western Europe recorded in saga tales as far back as 1500 BC. It was in hurling that the Irish hero Cuchulain made his name when, as a boy of twelve, he did a Stanley Matthews on the hurlers of the King's court and played them off the field. Some ancestral Celtic memory could trigger off an interest in hurling among EEC countries if it continues to have general presentation on television networks.

One innovation could help tremendously to popularise the game on an international level. A luminous ball which would scorch through the air and solve a serious spectator problem which is following the flight of the ball as it whizzes between hurls. Psychedelic hockey.

12th September, 1976

The Vasalopp – skiing at the edge of the world

The trees are still like a Japanese painting. Slim ribs of red slink through the duck-egg green of the sky. It is 7 am in Dalarna, in Northern Sweden. 10,740 skiers are about to begin a seventy mile cross-country race, the Vasalopp, which takes place each Spring. What happens next is like an acid trip. You see reds, greens, golds, oranges, purples, yellows flash in front of your eyes as the track suits of 10,000 skiers explode into movement. You feel the wind in your face created by the ski force as it hurtles across the flat field. Somewhere in the midst of this mass of molten colour is the King of Sweden. He has decided to join in the race. It is in fact called after his predecessor King Gustav Vasa, who after trying to rouse the townsmen of Mora against the Danes in 1521, was heading for Norway, when two yeomen caught him at Sälen and brought him back to lead the people. The race today is from Sälen to Mora, the other way around. And this is the first time a King has been over the course.

I had flown British Airways to Stockholm in 2¼ hours, over 900 miles. Up here many thousands of people were going to cover 70 miles without any mechanical aid whatever. Unless you have seen it in action, it is impossible to imagine how fast a man can go across country on skis. This race was won last year by a skier who reached an average of 17 miles an hour, a phenomenal speed when you consider it was done over a flat surface with only small eminences in between.

As it is, we have to go at quite a lick in our bus to catch up on the skiers at the first stop at Risberg. As the bus races along, you can see the skiers weaving in and out of the trees like insects. The cross-country movement requires perfect co-ordination of arms and legs. The skiers use ski sticks to pull them along as their legs slide forward in a way a little like the movement of roller skating, except that the ski doesn't rise from the ground.

We just made it to Risberg before the skiers arrived. Here there are great cauldrons of delicious blueberry soup, ready to be served to the skiers as they come by. Suddenly there's a shout and the first few come into sight whizzing along the flat. There are two Swedes, a Finn and a Russian. As they go past they grab their cups of blueberry soup, and soon the psychedelic stream has started with the colours flashing past your eyes in a way that reminds you of strobe lighting at the Electric Circus in New York.

I am watching out for Stig Bölling who is seventy-four. This is his fortieth competition, and he has skied 800 miles in preparation for this year. We have to leave before he arrives. The radio says that he is up with the third group.

A lone Englishman is competing. He is also with this group, Michael Jeneid. I haven't been able to find the Scottish competitor yet, Donald Ferguson. There are 176 Swiss competitors, 6 Russians and 100 Norwegians, as well as Austrians, Germans and French.

There are two more points along the route where we can watch the skiers coming in. But we will only have time to take in one of them as the skiers are going so fast. Most of the time you can see them from the road. Then they vanish in the forest.

At Evertsberg, the Finn, the Swede and the Russian are still neck and neck. From now on it will be much easier. There is a gentle slope of about 30 miles down to the town of Mora where the finish is a flat plain about a mile long on which the skiers will come in. We wait at the finishing post and watch as the leaders come into focus like polka dots on the white snow. They shoot through a tunnel of cheering spectators who line the route on either side. A charming touch is a Swedish cheer squad. This consists of a group of tiny angelic faced girls with their faces framed in golden curls who cry 'Heja, Heja', in fragile imitation of their American prototypes as they dance out to meet the winner. Surprisingly it is a Russian, Ivan Garanin. It seems very sporting of the Swedes to cheer the traditional enemy. He has won in 4 hours 30 minutes and 34 seconds. The heavy snow has slowed up the time. A wreath is placed on his shoulders as he makes a short speech from the platform. A Finn and a Swede have come in just behind him. Later at a press conference he comes in heavily guarded by politicals. He accuses someone, whom he will not name, of changing their skis during the race, which is illegal. This seems unnecessary since he has won. Three men with enormous backs in front of me look at him anxiously and make glottal sounds in his direction. I wondered had they told him to make this excuse in case he lost, and had forgotten to tell him not to make it if he won.

Down below, the skiers are still coming in. They will be arriving for the next seven hours. Meanwhile Nordic organisation is under way. Each of the 10,740 skiers has had his gear collected at the start in Sälen. Fifteen articulated lorries had collected it and set off within minutes. Now 10,740 bags were laid out nearby in immaculate order. This is the Swedish way. They had served 10,000 litres of blueberry soup, 15,000 litres of lime juice and 32,000 oranges, and 22,400 buns during the race. The tables these were served from, if they were laid out end to end, would have reached 520 metres. Each skier as he came in has had his time taken and will get a certificate for finishing.

At two o'clock Stig Bölling arrives. His time is 7 hours 9 minutes. At seventy-four years of age, he has covered seventy miles at almost ten miles an hour, some golden oldie. It doesn't seem to have taken a feather out of him. I caught up with him as he walked to the changing rooms. What would he do next? 'Begin training for next year,' he said with a grin. For the summer he would run eight miles a day through the Dalarna woods.

As I walked back to the finishing gate, I caught a glimpse of a magic name, on the front of the building beside the track: Anders Zorn, Sweden's only modern painter of world class, who lived in Mora. Inside the museum were the famous nudes, sensuous Nordic girls peeping through the trees, Maid Marion in the greenwood without a stitch. The Swedes were puzzled when these paintings caused a scandal at the turn of the century. For them, nakedness was a part of the nature they worshipped.

Outside there is a terrific roar. I run out. The King is coming up the straight looking very fit indeed. The cherubic little girls are in ecstasies of 'hejas'. He skies well and looks quite anonymous hurtling along among the plebs. Next to him is fifty-four-year-old Bengt Lauritz, a school teacher. The King with a sweating face grins at him as he passes the finishing gate. 'Thanks for the spar,' he says.

There are almost five thousand skiers to come in behind the King. They will arrive in clusters hour after hour. They come from every background. Svante Lindgvist is a vet, whom I talked to the night before at the Högfjälls Hotel in Sälen. He is sixty-four and it is his first Vasa Race. Ron Torrell is a businessman from Boras, the Manchester of Sweden. He was determined to beat 5½ hours, he told me before he went out. He comes in at 5 hours 20 minutes.

As the Northern night closes in the last skier comes in at 12 hours 57 minutes, a long time on skis if you are not in it for the money.

What is the motive that drives them for hours across the snow plains?

Is it the Nordic belief that alone in the hills and lakes you may find the answer to life? Dalarna is still the healing well for the bruised soul of modern Sweden. This yearning for something beyond the soporific of social security is caught by an early Dalarna poet, J. O. Wallin, and quoted by Bergman in his *Wild Strawberries*. I liked it so much I have had a shot at turning it into English.

Where is the Friend, that everywhere I am seeking,
When daylight comes my longing grows for Thee King.
When day departs I have not found my Master,
Though the heart beats faster.

I hear His Voice where summer winds are breathing;
Where forests sing, and where the river's seething.
Its splendour fills me, and where that Voice is
My heart rejoices.

Be strong my soul, hope, pray, surrender.

Your Friend beckons; soon you'll taste how tender
His Love can be; and sink upon His Bosom;
And never loose Him.

20th March, 1977

The jogging boom

'FAG!' they would scream at me ten years ago when I walked through New York's Central Park on a Sunday swinging my hips in race-walking style. I had to go fast, or I would have been mugged. At that time there were few walkers and no runners in the park. Now it has become a haven, a leafy, lush bower with a backdrop of Scottish baronial, and surrealistic skyscrapers climbing into phosphorescent sunsets. Elderly people lie on the grass in the sun. Children play without fear of being molested.

Jogging has worked this change. At weekends and on some weekdays, cars are banned in the park. The roadways then become jammed with joggers, cyclists, roller skaters, all on exercise trips. You see whole families, the father on a bicycle, the daughter on skates and the mother jogging. A guy with an Afro-cut that with a little wind resistance could make him airborne, goes by. An ancient 'wino' moves at an incredibly slow pace, holding up the front of his trousers. A character who calls himself 'The Rolling Machine', and listens to music on headphones while he skates, occasionally does somersaults between waltzes.

Jackie Onassis, Governor Carey, Jill Clayburgh, Dustin Hoffman are regular park joggers. The official figures indicate that serious crime – mugging, rape, assault – has decreased by one-third in the park.

'I've no doubt that this has been accomplished by closing the park to cars,' said parks commissioner Gordon Davis. 'People feel safe with human beings on two legs around. An impersonal object speeding through is no help.'

Lasse Viren, Finland's Olympic gold medallist, won a 10-kilometre race organised in Central Park by the New York Road Runners' Club in 29 min 13 secs. He was competing against 4,500 other runners, all of whom finished, including seventy-eight-year-old Herman Wallace, Mrs Adrienne Solmini, sixty-two, and Paul Mason, eleven, who last year ran a Marathon in 2 hrs 53 mins.

Afterwards a competitor colleague from *The Times* office in New York, still wearing her drenched tracksuit, said:

'I never ran till I came to New York. Now I intend to run in the New York Marathon next autumn.'

She produced her running schedules for the next four months. If she keeps to them, Rosie will run a Marathon next October in company with such intrepid New Yorkers as Dick Traum, who last year ran the race on one leg in 7 hours 24 minutes, and Miguel Paros, who is blind.

Central Park joggers came into their own during the transit strike. More than 2,000 citizens ran to work each morning carrying haversacks containing their office clothes on their backs. Judge Jim Jeffs, who weighs 21 stones, ran seven miles to his chambers, and said he had never felt better in his life. There is talk of having shower facilities built in to new office blocks.

A survey has shown that more than 18 per cent of Americans run at least once a week, an indication that jogging is losing its middle-class image and getting across to blue-collar workers who don't work at jobs involving physical labour. There are even running 'bums' who drop out of society and devote their time to improving their Marathon figures.

Sports shops are booming. Amateur athletes like Marty Liquori (who owns the Athletic Attic in Gainesville, Florida) have become rich. Besides an infinite variety of jogging shoes and running shoes, you can buy wristbands with a wallet-pouch built in, and an aerosol-powered device with a supersonic shriek to scare the hell out of nosey bow-wows. Also amassing wealth are foot specialists – pediatrists is the word – who claim to cure athletic injuries speedily and get you back to your favourite addiction in no time. One 'expert' told John Carlos, third in the 1968 Olympic 200 metres, that he had been running wrongly all his life, which was why his knee was bothering him, and Carlos humbly set about relearning how to run.

Once the automobile ruled in the States. You were a nut if you ran, or even walked. Why the change? Is it the well-known American predilection for cult? Probably not. Jogging remains popular because it makes people feel better. Dr George Sheehan, who finished 189th in the Central Park 10-kilometre race, has summed up his reason for running, and it could well represent the inner feelings of thousands of others:

'I want to bring back my body to become a total man . . . to be able to say, "I have found my hero, and he is me".'

20th April, 1980

Samuel Beckett man of letters – and sport

This Spring, Nobel Prize winner, Samuel Beckett, celebrates his seventieth birthday. Beckett, apostle of gloom, is not associated in the public mind with sport. But at Trinity College, Dublin, he was a first-class cricketer and he won his colours for cricket, boxing and rugby as a schoolboy at Portora, a 'brilliant' scrum half according to the school magazine.

The Trinity side that he played for is generally regarded as one of the best ever there. It included George McVeagh, capped for Ireland at tennis, squash and hockey as well as cricket, and Mark Sugden, the international rugby scrum half, famous for selling the dummy.

Was there any significance in the first four weeks of the cricket season of 1925 when Sam Beckett came into the Trinity XI? Grey gloom enveloped College Park each Saturday and for the only time in history, four successive matches were cancelled because of rain.

But the sun shone the following week for Trinity Week where Beckett had his first outing as a bowler and bat. Against Leinster Cricket Club the week after he was bowled for 61 by a gentleman who, when I mentioned the feat to him, asked me what Beckett was doing these days.

'Come and meet Sam,' said Jack McGowran one night in Paris. Beckett used McGowran as his leading man because of his darting rabbit face, marvellous furtive eyes, and frenzied voice, perfect for the Gospel of the Lost.

Jack, who had been Irish high jump champion, said it would do Sam good to hear the latest about Irish sport. We met him in the Closerie des Lilas. A face like an Aztec chieftain cut into a cliff; eyes that withdrew so far behind his glasses you felt if you looked too close, you mightn't come back again.

Life is real, life is earnest; and suddenly like a lamp switched on it was a face in a Dublin pub. We had begun talking about sport – the centre of gravity in the high jump which McGowran demonstrated over a chair while Beckett looked on with delight. Then we discussed cycling, running, boxing.

'Do you either of you remember Dickie Lloyd, the marvellous out half in the twenties?'

We didn't but Beckett remembered him.

'He once dropped a goal among a tangle of players inside his own half.'

Recently on the stage McGowran had sent the audience into convulsions with a passage from Beckett about a man counting stones in his pocket, the high noon of the absurd.

'I had, say, sixteen stones, four in each of my four pockets, these being the two pockets of my trousers and the two pockets of my great coat. . . . I replaced it in the right pocket of my great coat by a stone from the right pocket of my trousers, which I replaced by a stone from the left pocket of my trousers.'

I longed to ask what umpire Beckett had in mind; but I didn't want to risk the return of the Aztec look.

He mentioned his swimming relatives. Jim Beckett, his uncle, had been a heroic figure in Irish swimming when I was young.

> 'Dockrell, Taggart, Beckett, where
> Are the men I worshipped there?
> Some still rub the pink flesh dry
> Some have laid their towels by.'

The last time Sam had been in Dublin he had gone to visit two of these Olympian figures, a husband and wife.

'They had had their legs amputated.'

His eyes looked sad.

The play we had just seen was about a man and wife immured in dustbins.

Fifty-five years before Beckett had stood at the crease in the College Park in Trinity Week, another apostle of gloom had starred at the College Races. Bram Stoker, author of *Dracula* had become a national hero when he won the four and seven miles races in front of a crowd of 30,000 while bookies shouted the odds at the edge of the track.

But Bram, unlike Sam, did not keep up his interest in sport. There is no mention of any sport in his story of the thirsty Count – though it could be said that he carried his bat.

It's hard to see the authors of *Waiting for Godot* and *Dracula* against the background of the College Park. It is no place for Gothic gloom; but a bower of beauty in the city's heart where in a fine summer bumble bees stumble drunkenly across the cricket crease and pigeons grumble in the trees to drown the noise outside.

Another student who was at Trinity with Stoker and was an old boy of Beckett's school, avoided the place like the plague.

'I refuse to play cricket,' said Oscar Wilde when he came up to Trinity from Portora. 'The postures are indecent.'

22nd February, 1976

The creative mind and exercise

It is well recognised that creative artists are subject to melancholy. Exhausted by the frenzy of creation, they can experience what is known as 'the blacks'. In recent years, many creative people have discovered exercise as an antidote to the mental fatigue associated with imaginative output. Since 1964 Sir Laurence Olivier, for instance, has been doing weight-lifting for an hour before he goes on stage, and claims that it has a beneficial effect on his performance:

'I am a very good boy about my exercise,' he says, 'I do it scrupulously and regularly.'

Norman Mailer, weaving his arms in hooks and jabs like an articulated spider in P. J. Clarke's Bar, New York, told me:

'I have to go through my daily boxing routine at Cus d'Amato's gym to clear my mind.'

Tom Lehrer, satirist and composer of *Tomfoolery*, says:

'Yes, exercise makes me feel good. Not jogging or the Canadian Air Force exercises, which I hate. I tap dance for an hour every day and love it. When I realise I'm doing exercise as well, it kills two birds with the one stone.'

The novelist and playwright, Edna O'Brien, runs twice round her favourite square, and also does yoga at home.

'Any exercise that moves the body moves the brain,' is how she puts it.

Among other creative people who are into exercise are writers Kurt Vonnegut and Gore Vidal, and Ian Holm the actor.

But though exercise is currently in fashion, long before

jogging shoes and track suits came on the scene, there were writers who used it as an aid to creation. Jonathan Swift, author of *Gulliver's Travels*, was the first literary jogger. As far back as 1720 he wrote a letter priding himself on being the best walker in Dublin. He was so keen on exercise that when it was too wet to go outside he used to jog up and down the stairs in St Patrick's Cathedral Deanery with a servant standing at the bottom to count the repetitions, till His Reverence had covered eight miles; he claimed it cured his melancholia.

Bernard Shaw was another who believed in the value of exercise as a mind blower. He could cycle fifty miles on a week-end, swim every day in the Royal Automobile Club pool, besides going for eight mile walks.

'Shaw believed exercise purified the thought processes,' Michael Holroyd, his official biographer tells me. 'He actually claimed to have solved the problem of acquired habits while learning to ride his bicycle.'

Another passionate devotee of exercise was Yukio Mishima, the Japanese writer, one of the major novelists of the century. At thirty-two, with twenty novels behind him, Mishima believed he was spun out, unable to write any more. Then he discovered exercise, and took up boxing, weight-lifting, jogging, martial arts.

'Were I not able to renew my creaking skeleton five times a week,' he wrote, 'thanks to exercise coursing blood and creating sweat, I would have long ago become a corpse in spirit.'

Though Mishima did become an actual corpse when he committed ritual suicide at the age of forty-two, it seems clear from his writing that the benefits he got from exercise postponed for some years the fulfilment of what was a built-in death wish. Ernest Hemingway and Ezra Pound used to get the blood coursing through their veins with regular boxing sessions in Paris in the twenties. Hemingway used to boast of sparring with Larry Gains, but would get murderous if anyone mentioned the Canadian writer, Morley Callaghan, a useful man with his props, who put Hem down with a right hook one day when they were sparring. This damaged Hemingway's macho image so much that he chucked boxing and took up bull fighting to soothe his ego.

The Bauhaus group of Gropius, Schlemmer, Kandinsky and Klee used exercise as a preparation for creative work. First thing in the morning the great colourist Johannes Itten would put his class through breathing and vibrator exercises to stir up the mind.

Is there a scientific basis for what these creative people have discovered by instinct, I asked Dr Malcolm Carruthers, Director of Clinical Laboratory Services at the Maudsley Hospital, who has done experiments with top-class athletes. He believes that under stress of exercise athletes release a hormone 'which stimulates pleasure centres in the nervous system'. Dr Ronald Lawrence, Assistant Clinical Professor of Psychiatry at the University of California in Los Angeles, goes further.

'Last year we did a series of experiments on runners at Sadia, New Mexico,' he told me, 'and we found that after exercise the hormone endorphin, endogenously generates a morphine-like substance in the bloodstream.'

I asked him would this mean that exercise produced a similar 'high' to a shot of morphine?

'Yes, it does. But it's self-generated as long as you keep up the exercise – even minimal exercise. That's why I think so many people are addicted to jogging. Manic depression is as common these days as colds and these people are self-treating themselves with exercise.'

There is, then, hard scientific evidence that should encourage creative artists to do regular exercise as an antidote to the wear and tear of their trade. Oscar Wilde, Modigliani, Utrillo, Dylan Thomas, Brendan Behan, John Barrymore, Jack Kerouac, are among the writers and painters who died of drink or drugs before middle age. If they had been made aware of the self-generating restorative inside them released by exercise, might not their overweight and tortured bodies have been consigned less quickly to the tomb?

9th April, 1981

Illegal violence in sport

A rare prosecution for assault on the field of play will be brought this year when a player from Caerphilly rugby union club third XV will be charged with malicious wounding during a match against a borstal team at Usk in Wales.

It seems unfair that a prosecution for assault should be initiated in small-time rugby, when there have been notorious incidents in international soccer and rugby and, this year alone, at least two televised cases of assault between first division footballers.

Many sports involve violent contact which would amount to criminal assault if it took place off the field. It is the application of the legal maxim 'Volenti Non Fit Injuria' that makes this possible. If a player agrees to violence being used against him before going on to the field or in to the boxing ring he cannot complain then if it is used. For instance, a rugby tackle would be an assault and battery except that the two teams have agreed beforehand to dispense with the legal penalties. In boxing two athletes continually assault each other over a number of rounds but each has consented to this.

A vital provision in this dispensation in the law, however, is that it only applies as long as the players remain within the rules. For instance, if a rugby or soccer player punches an opponent he is liable both civilly and criminally. If a boxer were to kick his opponent or if it could be shown that he deliberately hit below the belt, he could be both sued and prosecuted.

In cricket a bowler who injures an opponent by aiming deliberately at him instead of at the wicket could be liable to prosecution. An extreme example would be a tennis player who drove a ball at an opponent hitting him deliberately in the eye. For common assault an accused can get a year's imprisonment under the Offences against the Person Act of 1861. If the skin is broken in the assault the offence is malicious wounding, and it carries with it a prison sentence of up to five years.

Recently, punching and kicking have become increasingly prevalent in rugby and soccer. In international matches between Wales and Ireland in 1969 and 1977 there were incidents in which two Irish players were knocked out by perfect boxing punches in full view of millions of TV watchers. The assaults did not interfere with the international careers of the players concerned.

The reason why assault on the rugby field has not been previously prosecuted is probably something to do with tradition. Rugby was once a gentleman's game, providing ample opportunity for violent contact within the rules. But gentlemen didn't take advantage of the rules to kick and punch. This is not so any longer.

It is quite clear from interviews with international players (especially those who have been on Lions tours) that Common Law assaults are prevalent in the modern game. In a TV interview some time ago a famous Lions forward let it be known that the motto on tour was, 'get your intimidation in first'.

The Rugby Union, anxious to preserve the tattered remnant of the old boy image, have not been as open as they might about this trend in the game. International players had it made known to them that their rugby careers could be affected if they discussed with journalists the question of dirty play on tour.

In recent years there have been a number of civil actions taken by players who have been injured as a result of a legal assault on the field. In December a French player, Armand Clerc, had a decree of nearly £8,000 given against Michel Palmie the French international, whom Clerc claimed had partially blinded him in a match in May 1975. That the French Rugby Union are taking the matter of violence seriously is indicated by the fact that a police prosecution was instigated against Douglas Sheck who plays for Narbonne and who had injured a player with a late tackle. He was convicted last month. In America recently the National Basketball Commissioner, Larry O'Brien, fined a player $80,000 for punching an opponent and partially paralysing him.

A distinct advantage of having a case tried in the courts instead of by a committee of a sports organisation is that the accused person will have the benefit of those procedures which the law has devised to get at the truth. He would be able to plead for instance that he had acted in self-defence when hitting his opponent. If proved this would provide a complete defence. In mitigation of his offence he could plead aggravation, either that he was himself assaulted first or that he was incensed by a verbal comment. An accused player could call witnesses and have the opportunity of cross examining those appearing for the other side, a procedure which might not be available at an inquiry held by a sports organisation.

Illegal violence in sport can only have the worst possible effect on the community. It is time for the Director of Public Prosecutions to direct his attention to the problem. After all why should a boy in Liverpool who punches somebody in the head in a street fight get a prison sentence while an educated 'gentleman' who does the same in the rugby field go scot-free?

12th February, 1978

New York's 'Guardian Angels'

These days the New York subways have become a jungle. In Brooklyn a man about to board a train was shot with a bow and arrow. When a policeman persisted in making a kid pay his train fare the charming youth simply pulled out a revolver and shot him. One man has used a meat cleaver on passengers on four occasions. When I asked a New York Assembly man, Sean Walsh, were things as bad as they seemed, he replied:

'They're worse. It reminds me of Chaka Impis sweeping Africa. Urban society is being ripped apart.'

Curt Sliwa decided to do something about the situation since the city authorities apparently had failed. He founded the 'Guardian Angels', a group of youths who ride the trains protecting passengers. They use no weapons but are all trained in Martial Arts. When they capture a criminal they hold him till the police arrive. Their approach is quite legal and is termed 'a citizen's arrest'.

Sliwa, a handsome John Travolta type who is twenty years of age, described one of these arrests.

'We were riding the "Muggers' Express" – that's the last train to Brooklyn. There's these two guys with their radio turned up so that no one could hear themselves talking. The driver came out and asked them to turn it down as he couldn't hear his signals coming in. They spat at him and turned it up louder. I said, "Don't you guys understand English" but all they did was to curse us out and pull a knife on us. So me and Jerry Munro moved in and we had them down in a few seconds. We handcuffed them to the strap hangers until the cops came round.'

Another night Sliwa and Jerry Munro found a man raping a girl at Columbus Circle on 57th which is only a couple of hundred yards from some of New York's poshest hotels.

'He tried to rip my jugular with a broken bottle but I just got on his back like a turtle so he couldn't move till Jerry got the cops.'

I rode the subways with eight 'Guardian Angels' on the 'Muggers' Express' to get the flavour of what they were at. We boarded a train at 10 pm. The 'angels' were all under twenty years of age. Carlo, George, Damon, Elijah, were some of their names. Of Italian, Black, Armenian and Puerto Rican racial background, they were a fair New York mix. At the token booth the guard signalled them through. It's a sign of the status they have received that the 'Angels' don't have to pay subway fares. They are recognisable by their red berets which, I was to find out, play an important part in their strategy.

Each 'Angel' travels in a separate train carriage. When the train stops at a station they get out for a second and signal to each other whether everything is okay in the carriage or not. As luck would have it nothing particular occurred on this journey. Carlo, sensing that I might have been a little disappointed, asked did I want to see what would have happened if something went wrong in our carriage. I told him to go ahead. At the first station on the way back, as soon as the train stopped, he stepped on the platform and took off his red beret. In a few seconds a scarlet avalanche engulfed the carriage as the other 'Angels' came flying down the train through the connecting doors to where Carlo was. They seemed a little put off to find there was nothing up, but he explained it was only a 'demo' for my benefit.

They promised to take me to an initiation the following day. A sixteen-year-old was undergoing a test for admission to the group. Next afternoon two 'Angels' called for me and drove me into the heart of Chinatown. There in a barrack-like gym two very tough ex-Army instructors were putting about forty youths through a fierce schedule of karate and other forms of martial arts. In the corner sat a rather slight, somewhat nervous looking boy. His name was Cesar Aviles and he was a candidate for the night's test. Cesar was sixteen years of age. I was the first journalist to be present at an initiation and I sensed something of the atmosphere of a tribal rite. As soon as the class was over the instructors signalled to Aviles. I didn't envy him. Two lines of 'Angels' now stood facing each other in the middle of the gym. It was Cesar's job to step into the tunnel between them and fight his way out. He stood there with his arms in the martial arts position and then moved forward. It seemed impossible that he could even make a yard's progress as each 'Angel' lashed out. But Cesar bounced off his assailants like a spinning top, shot through gaps like a scrum-half bent double, warded off chops and kicks with his arms and legs whirling like helicopter blades, till unbelievably, in four seconds, he was out the other side of the tunnel. Those guys who a second before had been trying to maim him now shook his hand. He had made it as a 'Guardian Angel'. From now on he could use the skills he had acquired as a means to protect the public.

One of the advantages that the 'Guardian Angels' have had in establishing themselves with the New York public is that their founder and spokesman, Curt Sliwa, has an upper class background. He was at a prep school, the equivalent, if there is one in the US, of going to an English public school and was headboy and captain of football and baseball at the exclusive academy where he was educated. Sliwa has ensured that there is no semblance of discrimination in selecting his troops. Boys from every racial group are represented and there are girl 'Guardian Angels' who have been admitted after passing the test. Deaf mutes have turned out to be ideal candidates since they can't hear the harassment as they move in silently to nail a robber. The 'Angels' give protection to anyone regardless of race, belief or outlook. When they heard that homosexuals were being mugged in Central Park they sent up a group to deal with the problem and succeeded in reducing drastically the number of attacks. Curt Sliwa is proud of the fact that the 'Guardian Angels' always act in defence of innocent people and have never resorted to weapons or overkill.

'Seventy-two citizen arrests without a single member of our group being brought to court shows the discipline we have.'

Though the Lieutenant Governor of New York has pub-
licly backed them, there have been inevitable yells from
certain police officials and politicians that approval of the
'Guardian Angels' will lead to 'vigilanteism'. But Assembly
man, Sean Walsh, reflects the attitude of the vast majority of
the public when he says:

'The police have shown they can't cope with subway
violence. They'd rather bring Maoris from New Zealand
than accept civilian help here. These boys have found a legal
way to reduce the crime rate on the subways. They should be
let do it their way.'

A song for sport

You can see Tommie Bracken, a Dublin street poet, selling his sporting ballads in the pubs. He is in the national tradition of perpetuating sport in verse. Though a fervent Irishman, he is, nevertheless, on England's side as long as they are playing against the foreigner.

> It was the day of jubilation
> It was the day of celebration
> It was the day of palpitation
> At Wembley Park.
>
> It was the day of Geoff Hurst
> It was the day old England burst
> With excitement and enlightenment
> At Wembley Park.

Arkle's success brought a whole string of ballads in its wake. The one you hear most often in the pubs, though, is Dominic Behan's.

> Oh it happened in the springtime
> of the year of '64.
> When Englishmen were making
> plans and fivers by the score.
> He beat them in the flat race,
> he beat them o'er the jumps,
> A pair of fancy fetlocks, he
> showed them all at once.

> But a quiet man called Dreaper
>   living in the Emerald Isle,
> Said a horse of yours called
>   Mill House surely shows a bit
>   of style,
> But I've a little fella, and Arkle
>   is his name,
> Put your money where your
>   mouth is and then we'll play
>   the game.

When they went away the Irish took the tradition of sporting ballads with them. Once when I was competing at a sports meeting at the Ibrox I was sure I heard some Glasgow Celtic supporters, who were waiting for 'futball', chant a ballad about Charlie Tully, the Celtic forward. Sean Fallon, the Celtic assistant manager, told me recently that he'd been unable to trace such a ballad, but there is the glorious one about another Celtic player, John Thomson, the goalie who was killed by a kick forty-four years ago this month:

> On the fifth day of September
> 'Gainst the Rangers club he played.
> From defeat he saved the Celtic,
> Ah, but what a price he paid.

> The ball comes on the centre's toe
> But John runs out and dives,
> The ball rolls by, but John lies still,
> For his club this hero died.

> So play up Glasgow Celtic,
> Stand up and play the game,
> For in your goal a spirit stands,
> Johnny Thomson is his name.

> Farewell my darling Johnny,
> Prince of players we must part,
> No more we'll stand and cheer you
> On the slopes of Celtic Park.

A high proportion of Irish sporting ballads refer to boxing. It was through victory in this sport that the Celt could assert his superiority over the Saxon. The best-known boxing ballad is about Dan Donnelly's victory over the Englishman, Cooper, at Donnelly's Hollow in Kilcullen in 1810. But from a sport lover's point of view there is better detail in the account of Paddy Murphy's victory over Johnny Batts, the English bully, at Moyvalley:

> Murphy, like a thrasher, to his
>   work he then began,
> Poor Johnny Batts he felt the
>   smart, the blood from him it ran,
> The blows were hot and heavy,
>   he received with right good will,
> And instead of English good
>   roast beef, of Murphy's got his fill.

Even more impressive is Miss Jane Murphy, who beat the cobwebs out of a German lady in New York:

> But now the time of trial comes,
>   Jane coming to her ground,
> With might came to her fight
>   upon the second round.
> The German dame fought actively,
>   they both came to a close,
> Down slap-bang goes the German,
>   giving claret from the nose.
>
> The German girl got savage like when
>   twice she was knocked down,
> But Jane fought her close and keen
>   up to the eleventh round.
> The German with a favourite box
>   J. Murphy did surprise,
> She lay for half a minute still
>   – she's dead, was all their cries.

Jane, however, made a come-back in the last round to knock out her opponent. Would Germaine Greer have put up a better show in the cause of Women's Lib?

Ireland's national game, hurling, has had numerous ballads written about it. One of these is the one-hundred-and-fifty-year-old *The Carrigaline Hurlers*, in which the balladeer uses the chiming assonance of Irish classical poetry, the vowels running in and out of the lines like a terrier after a rat. For instance, the last word of one line rhymes with a word in the middle of the next:

> First I'll extol stout Saunders, and after him brave LANDERS
> They behaved like great COMMANDERS; and next I'll
>   aggrandise
> O'Toomey and Mulcahy; two Carties, and Bat FAHEY
> O'Callaghan of RAHEY, and also Thomas Wise;
> O'Flinn, with head like CARROT; De Cogans, Jack and
>   GARRET,
> And Jordan, Welsh and BARRETT; on the plains of
>   Ownabwee.

It is widely held that the greatest of Irish sporting ballads is *The Bould Tadhy Quill*. Although it was written in 1886, it didn't become known outside Cork until after the Nazi war. I first heard it sung by an RAF group captain after a match with London Irish at Sunbury in the 'fifties. The ballad recounts the feats of a multi-talented Corkonian who performs the sort of athletic miracles that Wilson used to in the pages of the *Wizard*.

> At the great hurlin' match between Cork and Tipperary,
> 'Twas played in the Park by the Banks of the Lee,
> Our own darlin' boys were afraid of being beaten,
> So they sent for bould Tadhy to Ballinagree.
> He hurled the ball left and right in their faces,
> And show'd those Tipperary boys learnin' and skill,
> If they came in his way, shure he surely would brain 'em,
> And the papers were full of the praise of Thade Quill.

There was seemingly no event that Tadhy could not excel at.

> Brave Tadhy is known in all sorts of places.
> At the athletic meeting held out in Cloghroe,
> He won the long jump without throwing off his braces
> With twenty-three feet from the heel to the toe.
> At putting the shot there was a Dublinman foremost,

But Tadhy got up and exceeded him still,
And around he whole parish rang the wild ringin' chorus,
Here's luck to our Hero, the bould Tadhy Quill.

Tadhy Quill was a real person. I met his cousin, Denis McSweeney recently. But alas, Denis tells me that Tadhy was not the paragon the ballad describes. In fact, the real Tadhy never lifted a hurl nor jumped over a lath in his life. Denis says:

'He was a big shy fellow, lazy and easy-going. The ballad was made as a lampoon of him by Johnny Gleeson, another cousin. The thing is that Tadhy liked the ballad. He was a sort of iron fool; though if he felt they were mocking him too much, he'd get angry. There was a thin line to maintain, but generally he was pleased. Later the song became known as The North Cork Anthem, and was played before all the sports meetings there.'

Tadhy was even known to sing his own song – a sort of Walter Mitty with a supplied script.

Now that we know that the feats attributed to Tadhy never took place, should we have reservations about other sporting ballads? I think not. Ballads recapture the high elation of sport for the man with a glass in his hand. If the art is there, detail can be dispensed with.

14th September, 1975

Suzy Chaffee – beauty on skis

Suzy Chaffee was the No. 1 skier in the United States in 1967 and captained the US Olympic Girls' Squad in 1968. But now she has invented a new sport – free style skiing. It includes somersaulting on skis as well as choreography to music and presently is second only to football in American TV ratings. This year, demonstrating the new sport to a photographer from the staid *Town & Country* magazine, Suzy felt she wanted to take off her clothes. When the photograph of Suzy on skis but with nothing else on appeared in the magazine, the editor expected an outcry. Amazingly the blue rinse ladies were not antagonised. The combination of sport and nudity appealed to readers who would have cancelled their subscription had a photograph of a naked girl appeared in another context.

Of course, Suzy is helped by the fact that she has the looks of the classical All-American Girl; leggy (5 ft 9 in), blonde and with light blue eyes that actually seem to glow. If Louisa Alcott had written a novel about girls on skis, Suzy would have been the heroine.

She writes poetry too. But here she leaves the world of coffee-tables and ladies clubs. For, whisper, Suzy is a radical, closer to the acid and pot generation than to the silent majority. One of her poems urges athletes to find themselves and not remain just dumb jocks.

> Tell it like it is!
> That angry young athletes run in the
> shade of records

And bear false oaths to grey ideals
That keep the poor from health and
  ecstasy
While satellites make us reluctant
  witnesses.

She believes the amateur concept of the Olympics is out of date and wants professionals as well as amateurs to be allowed to compete together.

A top mannequin who modelled at the Paris Collection in 1972, she uses the money she makes to travel to Moscow, Belgrade, London, Paris, Tel Aviv and rally the athletes in support of her sports philosophy.

A measure of her success is that she has been co-opted onto the US Olympic Committee's Board of Directors, one of three women on it among fifty-seven men. Suzy is a great believer in doing her homework. She may turn up at a party draped in a wolfskin rug with not an awful lot on underneath and come over as a sex bomb – but she can also lecture on sexuality in sport at the sophisticated Esalen Institute in California.

Suzy showed up in Dublin a few weeks ago. I had met her in New York and she said she'd call me some day. She liked Ireland because she'd seen it in the movie, *Ryan's Daughter*.

She hit the Green Isle in the middle of a rain storm. Suzy just held her face up to it. 'Nature,' she breathed.

Ice maidens are rare in a country where women are noted for grey eyes and black hair. People stopped and stared at her as she walked through the streets. Suzy says she likes making men blush because blood to the face is good for the brain.

Waiting for a charity show I was taking part in to begin, she spent four hours in a cold Christian Brothers hall. No sweat – she just read a book. The Brothers did their nut over her. She wafted a sense of vitality into the celibate air which made sin seem irrelevant.

The day she left the sun came out. She lay on the grass in a public park and did her exercises. Those beautiful golden legs twirling in the air sent up pulse rates. As she shook the grass out of her hair Suzy said:

'Watching the trees grow takes me back to living. You've

got to let yourself bloom and follow your gut.'

At dinner that evening in a restaurant she asked me to play the 'knee game'. This meant putting my knees outside hers and letting her try and force her thighs open against pressure from me. The contest takes place under the table so people at other tables don't notice. The pressure was frightful because she has thighs like iron. Her eyes widened and her breath came in little spurts. A flush came to her peaches and cream cheeks. An onlooker might have thought I was whispering sweet nothings to her. Actually I was wondering if my sartorius muscle wouldn't snap like a rubber band. I did hold her, though. She seemed surprised.

'First time I've lost,' she gasped.

The taximan who drove us to the airport and listened to her chat on the way out was mesmerised.

'Jesus, that one's a mixture of Joan of Arc and Marilyn Monroe,' he said.

I recited to him a verse from Suzy's poem *Tell It Like It Is* and he wrote it down and said he'd give it to his wife.

> Tell it like it is!
> That women overpopulate for lack of
>   other physical skills,
> That sex machines replace loving muscles,
> That the mind has lost the body in a
>   neon maze
> And the masses sell out for happiness
>   promised in rainbow packages.

17th August, 1975

INDEX

Norton, George 34
Norton, Ken 74

O'Brien, Edna 118
O'Brien, Larry 123
O'Callaghan, Dr. Pat 11–12
O'Connor, Christy 84, 86
O'Flanagan, Dr. Kevin 45–8
O'Flanagan, Michael 48
O'Reilly, Brendan 24
O'Reilly, Tony ix
Olivier, Sir Laurence 83, 118
Olympics xiv–xvii, 10–11, 97, 113, 135
  1900 11
  1904 11
  1908 11
  1924 15
  1928 11, 15
  1932 14–15
  1936 xi, 10, 12
  1956 xvi
  1960 10
  1968 113, 134
  1980 45
  1984 16
  Montreal Disabled Athletics 17
Open, the 84–5

Packer, Kerry 98
Palmie, Michel 122
paraplegic athletics 17
Pareth, Benny 97
Parker, Frank 99
Paros, Miguel 113
Periton, Joe 50
Pfiffer 76
Pike, Victor 51
Pistre, Father Henri 27–30
Player, Gary 88
Plymouth Argyle 45
Portmarnock golf course 84
Pott, Johny 89
Pound, Ezra 119
Prat, Jean 29
push-ups 18

quadraplegia 31–3

Quill, Tadhy 132

Rathfarnam 87
Reifenstahl, Leni xi
Robinson, Ray 60
Roch, Peggy 59
Rockwell school xi
Rooke, Rev. C. V. 40
Rosebowl football team 97
Rowsome, Billy 104
Royal St. George's 85
rugby ix–xiv, xvii, 27–52, 82, 115, 122–3
running 15, 46, 118, 120
  see also jogging
Ryan, Paddy 11
Ryan, Rasher 88

St. Mary school xi
Sandhurst 82
Scannell, Father Sean 85
Schlemmer, Oskar 120
Scott, Bob 34–5
Segura, Pancho 98
Shamrock Rovers xviii
Sharkey, Jack 68
Sharpe, Richard 34
Shaw, Bernard 119
Sheck, Douglas 123
Sheehan, Dr. George 114
shot putting 15, 17–18
Shrewsbury school 15
skiing 107–11, 134–6
Sliwa, Curt 124–6
Smith 82
Smith, Cove 40
Smith, Gunboat 60
Smith, Ian 41
soccer xvii–xviii, 23, 45–8, 122, 128–9
Solmini, Adrienne 113
Somen 76
songs 128–33
Springboks 82
squash 52, 83, 115
Stampfl, Franz xiv–xvi
Stander, Ron 74
Stevens, Claude 17–19